Introduction to Claudia Rankine

LAKE FOREST
COLLEGE
PRESS

Introduction to Claudia Rankine

Kathy Lou Schultz

First published 2023 by Lake Forest College Press.

Carnegie Hall
Lake Forest College
555 N. Sheridan Road
Lake Forest, IL 60045

lakeforest.edu

Lake Forest College Press publishes in the broad
spaces of Chicago studies. Our imprint, &NOW Books,
publishes innovative and conceptual literature and serves
as the publishing arm of the &NOW writers' conference
and organization.

ISBN: 978-1-941423-08-0

Library of Congress Cataloguing-in-Publication data has been
applied for.

Printed in the United States

Contents

Introduction   1

1. Before *Citizen*: Lyric Subjectivity and the Language of
    Experience in Claudia Rankine's *Nothing in Nature is
    Private*   23

2. The Work of Silence in *The End of the Alphabet*   42

3. Contamination and "Poisoned Regrets": Mothers and Artists
    in Claudia Rankine's *PLOT*   67

4. Word, Image, Feeling: *Don't Let Me Be Lonely* and Social
    Documentary   91

5. Remaking the Social Body in *Citizen*   118

    Works Cited   157

Acknowledgments

Thank you to my editor, Robert Archambeau, for enduring patience and the opportunity to introduce Claudia Rankine's poetry, especially her earlier work, to audiences who may not have encountered it before. Thank you to the many people who sent me journal articles and other texts that I needed, but could not access, sometimes responding within minutes of my request. These people include Matt Hart, Jean-Phillipe Marcoux, and Jerrold Shiroma. I am highly appreciative of this community effort and if I have forgotten to mention other's names, please know that I am still very grateful. Thank you to Kat Moore for her copy of *Nothing in Nature is Private*, which is out of print. Thank you to Fowler Jones for research assistance. Thank you to the graduate students in my Major Authors in African American Literature seminar, for which I focused on Audre Lorde and Claudia Rankine, for your enthusiasm, insights, and willingness to follow my wild ride. Thank you to Ridvan Askin and Julius Greve for inviting me to speak about Claudia Rankine at the "Rethinking the North American Long Poem: Matter, Form, Experiment" conference at the University of Basel, Switzerland. Thank you to Terrence Tucker and Shelby Crosby for much-needed camaraderie. Thank you to the National Center for Faculty Development and Diversity for helping me with my writing practice and getting my life back. Thank you to the two peer reviewers whose careful readings and detailed commentaries helped me to make this a better book. Thank you to Brian for making the food, keeping the faith, and putting up with my general nonsense, and thank you to our very tall son and his very dry wit for making me laugh even when news of the world is not very funny. And thank you to friends, colleagues, poets, and scholars near and far who are part of my village.

A previous version of Chapter 1, "Before *Citizen*: Subjectivity and the Language of Experience in Claudia Rankine's *Nothing in Nature is Private*," appeared in the *Journal of Foreign Languages and Cultures* 3.1 (June 2019), 117-126. Grateful acknowledgement to Lauri Scheyer and all the editors.

Introduction

Claudia Rankine was born in Kingston, Jamaica, in 1963. She grew up in Kingston and the United States, immigrating with her parents at the age of seven to the Bronx, New York, where her father worked as a hospital orderly, and her mother as a nurse's aide (Lee). Her parents encouraged reading and studying poetry. "In Jamaica, Rankine's mother had memorised poems at school, which made her 'quite a big advocate' for poetry. The first poem Rankine knew was Emily Dickinson's 'Because I Could Not Stop For Death,' which her mother read to her a year after the move to the US" (Cocozza). Rankine attended Roman Catholic elementary and secondary schools in the Bronx (Serafin). She earned her undergraduate degree from Williams College in 1985 and her MFA in creative writing from Columbia University in the City of New York in 1993.

In addition to the early influence of Dickinson, Rankine names poet Adrienne Rich as a significant source of inspiration: "There was something about the way in which Rich addressed social issues from a very personal position that made me want to write. This strategy of bringing the historical, the current moment and the emotional landscape of the speaker into the poem attracted me from the very beginning" (S. Bell). Rankine read Rich, along with James Baldwin, as an undergraduate in the early 1980s. "As a nineteen-year-old, I read in Rich and Baldwin a twinned dissatisfaction with systems invested in a single, dominant, oppressive narrative. My initial understanding of feminism and racism came from these two writers in the same weeks and months" (Rankine, "Adrienne Rich's Poetic Transformations"). In Rich, Rankine found a model for wedding past and present political and emotional landscapes, or what Rich calls in *Blood, Bread, and Poetry: Selected Prose 1979-1985*, the "political world 'out there'" and the "supposedly private, lyrical world" (Rankine, "Adrienne Rich's Poetic Transformations"). In a similar manner, each of Rankine's books of poetry, though very different in form and style, investigates the polarization of public and private.

Despite what may look like a fairly seamless artistic trajectory, given her education and publishing history, Rankine's decision to become a poet was, in fact, undertaken after long contemplation. During a reading she gave at the 92nd Street Y in New York in 2015, Rankine discusses the time in her life when she had to choose between being a lawyer and being a poet. Working as a paralegal during the day, Rankine took writing workshops at the 92nd Street Y in the evenings, which helped to solidify her decision to commit to poetry ("Claudia Rankine Reads from Citizen at the 92nd Street Y"). In an interview with Paula Cocozza for *The Guardian*, Rankine explains that although her parents stressed reading and education, they were initially hesitant about her choice of careers. For a child of immigrants, [choosing to be a poet] was a huge decision," she says, "You don't become a poet if you want to make any money." Her parents were initially confused by her intended career, but the Master of Fine Arts in poetry led to a teaching post. "And once I got a job ..." she laughs, "once they saw that, yes, I could live without their help, they were OK" (Cocozza). From that first teaching job, Rankine went on to become a prolific and distinguished poet, playwright, editor, and professor.

Among her numerous awards and honors, Rankine is the recipient of the Poets & Writers' Jackson Poetry Prize and fellowships from the Lannan Foundation and the National Endowment of the Arts. In 2005, Rankine was awarded the Academy Fellowship for distinguished poetic achievement by the Academy of American Poets and in 2013 the Academy elected her a Chancellor. In 2016, she was named a United States Artists Zell fellow in literature and also received a MacArthur "Genius" Grant. Using the $625,000 award from her MacArthur Grant,

Rankine founded the Racial Imaginary Institute, "a moving collaboration with other collectives, spaces, artists, and organizations towards art exhibitions, readings, dialogues, lectures, performances, and screenings that engage the subject of race" ("The Whiteness Issue"). The Mission Statement of the Institute is as follows: "Because no sphere of life is untouched by race, the Institute gathers under its aegis an interdisciplinary range of artists, writers, knowledge-producers, and activists. It convenes a cultural laboratory in which the racial imaginaries of our time and place are engaged, read, countered, contextualized and demystified" ("The Whiteness Issue"). "Demystifying" whiteness is a central project at a time when whiteness often remains unscrutinized. Rankine went on to win a distinguished Guggenheim Fellowship in 2017, and in 2020, she was inducted into American Academy of Arts & Sciences.

Well-known for her best-selling and multiple award-winning book, *Citizen: An American Lyric* (Graywolf Press 2014), Rankine is the author of five books of poetry. In addition to *Citizen*, her collections of poetry are: *Don't Let Me Be Lonely: An American Lyric* (Graywolf Press 2004); *PLOT* (Grove Press 2001); *The End of the Alphabet* (Grove Press 1998); and *Nothing in Nature Is Private* (Cleveland State University 1994). *Just Us: An American Conversation* (Graywolf), a book of essays, was published in 2020. For *Citizen*, Rankine's numerous awards include the PEN Open Book Award, the PEN Literary Award, the NAACP Award, and the National Book Critics Circle Award for Poetry. Notably, *Citizen* was the first book ever to be named a finalist in both the poetry and criticism categories by the National Book Critics Circle, and *Citizen* holds the highly unusual distinction of being the only poetry book to be a *New York Times* bestseller in the non-fiction category.

Rankine's poetry books engage a wide variety of formal techniques and subject matter. Utilizing modes including the lyric and pastoral, Rankine's first book, *Nothing in Nature Is Private*

(1994), explores the history and multiple meanings of the term "American," including descriptions of American landscapes. In confronting the conception of "Americanness," the poems in *Nothing in Nature is Private* push against typical discourses of nation, as represented in American history and literature, and the power they represent. The poems transform the pastoral tradition into a Black pastoral, similar to the mode of Claude McKay's Shakespearean sonnets, which become vehicles for expressing Black revolutionary resistance, rather than examination of "timeless" concerns, such as love, beauty, or mortality. For Black poets, Camille T. Dungy argues, nature writing, including meditations upon trees—particularly trees in the American South—can lead to "a history steeped in often arbitrarily brutal and always dehumanizing racism" *and* "a renewed connection to the natural world," thus complicating the tradition of the pastoral that portrays often idealized visions of nature as "diversion" and a "construction of a culture that dreams, through landscape and animal life, of a certain luxury or innocence" (xxi). Rankine's employment of a Black pastoral enriches and complicates the history of the pastoral, while also introducing content that challenges the lyric's putative connection to timeless individuality.

A number of scholars have contributed to the expanding field of lyric studies, which analyzes the category of lyric poetry to comprehend how the form has historically evolved and engages fundamental questions concerning how poets and critics employ the form and term in the twentieth century. A brief overview of this scholarship enhances analysis of Rankine, whose engagement with form is central to her poetics. For example, Jonathan Culler, author of *Theory of the Lyric* (2017), argues that "the category of the lyric makes sense," and that "there is a Western lyric tradition created by poets themselves who read each other, who attempt similar things, even though these poems may be created in very different social and political circumstances" (Culler 7). Thus, "the singer to the lyre in ancient Greece and today's academic poet" share a common tradition (Culler 7). Culler sees the poem as an "event," or what he calls "the lyric now" (10). Therefore, what he calls lyric is "language that strives to be an event rather than a representation of an event" (13).

Virginia Jackson, on the other hand, maintains that "the lyric takes form through the development of reading practices in the nineteenth and twentieth centuries that become the practice of literary criticism," or what she terms "lyric reading," a theory she carefully develops in her monograph, *Dickinson's Misery* (2005) (Jackson 8). Beginning with analysis of examples from Dickinson's letters, one to her brother Austin, and ephemera, a leaf pinned to a piece of paper, Jackson demonstrates that editors transformed these into something recognizable as a "poem" with line breaks. Jackson illustrates that what we now receive as "lyric" is thus part editor-created fiction—not a stable form that exists through time. According to Jackson, such editorial and reading practices result in all kinds of texts (such as songs, elegies, and letters) being labeled "lyric," a practice so ubiquitous and yet vague that "lyric" becomes a synonym for poetry itself.

Culler also argues that "the model of lyric as intense expression of the subjective experience of the poet does not fit a great many poems, ancient or modern, and, more important, it leads away from the language of the poem to an experience of the poet, which a reader is supposed to try to reconstruct" (Culler 9). This way of reading—focusing on the expression of emotion by an individual lyric subject—is reinforced by some contemporary classroom pedagogies. For example, The Sixth Edition of *The Norton Anthology of Poetry* (2018), which many students encounter, defines "lyric" as "a short poem, with the original sense in Greek of being sung (as to a lyre). Today the term applies to a short poem in any meter or free verse, in which the expression of emotion, often by voice in the first person, is given primacy over narration" (Ferguson et al. A10). The emphasis upon "short" poems is rather vague, but this, as other standard definitions, separates lyric poetry from the epic, which is "long." The ways Rankine uses and defines lyric in her own work complicates the definition's emphasis on length, as well as on the individual's "expression of emotion."

The type of reading practices that focuses on reconstructing what the poet is supposedly feeling and experiencing, Culler argues, reduces all lyric poetry to "the dramatic monologue model" (9) in which the poet supposedly addresses the reader in their own voice. The practice also moves the reader away from focusing on analyzing the language of the poem or the ways it looks on the page. Poet and scholar Daniel Tiffany outlines some similar views, arguing that "today's eroding, yet still dominant, model of lyric poetry...is oriented around notions of individual experience, feeling, and reflection—a paradigm often held to be a product of early Romanticism" (Tiffany, "Lyric Poetry and Poetics"). Analogous to Jackson, Tiffany demonstrates that "instituting a canon of lyric poetry that is presumed to comprehend and subsume all other genres of poetry," results in the problem of assuming that poetry itself is "equivalent to lyric" (Tiffany, "Lyric Poetry and Poetics").

For Tiffany, however, "Lyric poetry is an ancient genre, enduring to the present day, but it is not continuous in its longevity," showing that he, Culler, and Jackson form distinct historical lineages of the lyric (Tiffany, "Lyric Poetry and Poetics"). He argues that the belief in "the heightened experience, emotion, or reflection associated with lyric" that finds "expression in a correspondingly heightened register of language" produces what he calls "a reservoir of lyric diction." This type of "heightened" language sometimes echoes "the language of prayer, hymns, and biblical verse but also the legacy of classical Antiquity" characteristics of which, according to Tiffany, include "ornamentation, artifice, abstraction, figures of speech, archaism, and subjective feeling or sentimentality" (Tiffany, "Lyric Poetry and Poetics"). In the eighteenth century, however, lyric poetry incorporated "unfamiliar vocabularies" which, Tiffany argues, "was accompanied by generic instability and by new transactions between genres" (Tiffany, "Lyric Poetry and Poetics"). These include "the introduction of dialect, folk songs, and vernacular language into the lyric tradition" that are "derived from various marginal communities" (Tiffany, "Speaking in Tongues"). Tiffany argues for the need of poetry criticism that focuses on style, especially diction, as opposed to form.

African Americanist literary scholars have long studied African American vernacular styles (signifying, sermons, folktales, the ring shout), dialects (varieties of spoken African American English, slang, patois, idiolectical word play), African American verbal forms (call and response, the Dozens, the Boast), musical forms (African drumming, gospel, rhythm and blues, the blues, jazz, Hip Hop, sampling), African American grammatical formulations, and others in African American poetry. There is a large body of scholarship on these subjects.

There is also a growing body of work on "innovative" African American poetry, shown in the poetry collected by Aldon Nielsen and Lauri Scheyer in two anthologies: *Every Goodbye Ain't Gone: An Anthology of Innovative Poetry by African Americans* (Nielsen and Scheyer, *Every Goodbye Ain't Gone*); and, *What I Say: Innovative Poetry by Black Writers in America* (Nielsen and Scheyer, *What I Say*). Rankine's work is included in the latter. Among the many books of scholarship on this topic, Evie Shockley's *Renegade Poetics: Black Aesthetics and Formal Innovation in African American Poetry* carefully works to define "innovation," one example being African American women (Gwendolyn Brooks, Sonia Sanchez, Harryette Mullen) who "employ lyric stanzas in building poems of epic length, scope, or structure," thus "innovating" by combining forms (Shockley 16).

This illustrates the necessity of further defining the forms that are being used in combination. Rankine puts particular pressure on the term "lyric."

For Rankine, "the lyric is a place where feeling gets examined. It's traditionally grounded in the apprehensions and emotions of a subject. By coupling lyric with American, one takes the gesture into the public realm" (Rankine, "On Being Seen: An Interview with Claudia Rankine from Ferguson."). Acknowledging the traditional link between the lyric and supposedly private subjectivity, Rankine seeks to move these "private" emotions and concerns into public discourse, which she specifically acknowledges in the subtitles of her "American Lyric" books. When the term "lyric" is employed in this study of Rankine, it acknowledges that the lyric is often assumed to be a form of individual expression, while also analyzing how Rankine modifies this mode to address opposing categories, for example: nationalism and globalism, silence and speaking, stasis and motion, or the individual body and the social body, in addition to the public and private realms that she encountered when reading Rich. Thus, the lyric has modes that one may point to (the lyric "I," for example) but it is not a form that exists in a stable manner over time. Rankine's combinations and crossing of genres directly address the instability of form, as well as the inability of language itself to adequately express subjectivity. Her work also exemplifies African Americans' innovative use of inherited forms of poetry, remaking them to represent contemporary Black life.

A remarkable shift from the poems in her first book, in her second book, *The End of the Alphabet* (1998), Rankine follows in the lineage of poet Paul Celan in using a poetics of silence to engage a subjectivity estranged by unspeakable wounds. These poems challenge the formation of subjectivity itself, and thus lyric conventions. *The End of the Alphabet* focuses on traumas located in the female body, investigating how the concepts of aphasia and "hysteria" are intertwined with pregnancy loss, trauma, and death. These wounds are made visible through language as the self collapses. When "she" collapses, when the poet opens up grammar and syntax instead of sticking to accepted conventions, or when she does not "stitch" together a narrative façade, a new kind of sense can be made that more closely approximates subjectivity and experience than conventional lyric or narrative forms.

In moving away from narrative closure in *The End of the Alphabet*, Rankine's aim, as she describes it, is to "distress the reading experience" (Rankine, "Claudia Rankine" 150). In this process, words are "no longer markings to be skimmed over toward the close of an expected narrative... The reading experience then would be a journey into a process outside of the narrative plot-driven arc" (Rankine, "Claudia Rankine" 150-151). However, Rankine is not dispensing with the "self," she is taking a further step as she investigates how to render subjectivity even more intimately than in autobiographical or confessional poetry. "My desire [in *The End of the Alphabet*]," Rankine relates to interviewer Katie Lederer, "was to revise what it meant to be 'confessional' or autobiographical" (Rankine, "Claudia Rankine" 148). Thus, Rankine isn't eschewing the "self," but instead creating a new poetics of selfhood. Here again, Rankine is pushing the boundaries of literary forms and genres by questioning the way narrative and its "plot-driven arc" is constructed and employed.

Some narrative theorists place "narrative" in opposition to "lyric," as in the definition of lyric from the Norton anthology cited above. For example, Project Narrative at Ohio State University supposes that "narrative theorists study what is distinctive about narrative (how it is different from other kinds of discourse, such as lyric poems, arguments, lists, descriptions, statistical analyses, and so on)...Narrative theorists, in short, study how stories help people make sense of the world, while also studying how people make sense of stories" ("What Is Narrative Theory?"). The opening of the entry for "Narrative" in *The Routledge Dictionary of Literary Terms* states that narrative is "[t]he recounting of a series of facts or events and the establishing of some connection between them. The word is commonly restricted to fiction, ancient epics and romances or modern novels and short stories" (Childs and Fowler). Another explanation, a literary guide from Yale University Press, states that narratologists "frequently study the nature of plot (how and to what extent it recapitulates or circles back on itself, for example)" and "are engaged in a search for the essence of storytelling through an examination of the rules that govern, in any story, questions of problem and solution, beginning and ending, progress and obstruction" (Mikics). The commonalities here are on the essence of "story."

Thus, when Rankine wrote *PLOT* (2001), she was indeed challenging the limits of "story," and the essence of plot. *PLOT* is a book-length poem that examines relationships and individual identity within the bourgeoise family, in particular the contradictions, split identities, and conflicts associated with the multiple affiliations and responsibilities that women artists face when they become mothers. *PLOT* wrestles with sometimes irreconcilable identities through fragmented narratives stitched from lyric, dialogue, and prose. *PLOT* is distinctive because its larger formal structure (nine sections or months plus an Afterword) is in part predetermined by the subject—pregnancy and the birth of a child—and the book is written in conversation with outside texts, including two works by Ingmar Bergman (*Scenes from a Marriage*, a TV mini-series released in 1973, and the 1957 film, *Wild Strawberries*) and Virginia Woolf's novel *To the Lighthouse* from which Rankine borrows characters and themes. Throughout the poem, Rankine plays with and incorporates multiple meanings of "plot."

In *Don't Let Me Be Lonely: An American Lyric* (2004), the first of her "American Lyric" pairing, Rankine casts a light back upon the classification of lyric. *Don't Let Me Be Lonely* is also the first of her poetry books to contain a wide variety of multi-media images which participate in the American genre of the social documentary. The images include a small, cube-like television, an x-ray, photographs, maps, prescription labels, and a diagram of an artificial heart. The repeated image of television screens illustrates Rankine's investigation of media and representation. As a documentary poem that also draws attention to lyric modes, *Don't Let Me Be Lonely* examines illness (cancer, dementia, heart disease, HIV/AIDS) and dis-ease (loneliness, sadness, hopelessness) as both individual and social states of being and takes up, as an ethical question, the relationship of the self to others. In doing so, this "American Lyric" puts private feeling and ephemera into public view.

With *Citizen*, the second "American Lyric" book, Rankine explicitly seeks to enter public conversations about individual and systemic racism in order to encourage dialogue. The book crosses lyric and narrative forms. "Project Narrative" argues that:

> Narratives of all kinds are relevant to the field: literary fictions and nonfictions, film narratives, comics and graphic novels, hypertexts and other computer-mediated narratives, oral narratives occurring during the give and take of everyday conversation, as well as narratives told in courtrooms, doctors' offices, business conference rooms—indeed, anywhere. ("What Is Narrative Theory?")

Given that *Citizen* is made up of multiple accounts of experiences that actually took place in everyday places such as these, it is apparent why some readers approach *Citizen* as non-fiction, or narrative. Understood as a series of small stories, *Citizen* achieves a broader readership than Rankine's previous work, which may account, in part, for its popularity. But *Citizen* also ignites questions of form that are present in each of her previous books. It presents an opportunity to investigate the "single dominant, oppressive narrative" (in the previous examples of Rich and Baldwin), the formulation of a lyric subject, who gets the power to speak, and how stories are constructed and relayed. Form matters as both an expression of and intensification of content, using the page to reinforce connections, sounds, point of emphasis, and more. Choice of form can also continue or disrupt historical traditions, as poets seek to write marginalized subjects into literary canons.

In addition, having a text that can intimately engage readers with the experiences of individual and systemic racism is a crucial source for Americans facing an onslaught of police killings of Black men and women in situations that can begin as innocuous traffic stops. Visually, the book contains a series of prose blocks that have also been called a series of prose poems, but the book jumps genres as it also expands on the multi-media, visual reading experience of the social documentary. *Citizen* is a multi-media work that includes text, photographs, and full-color reproductions of contemporary art, as well as poem scripts that form the basis for the "Situation" video poems that Rankine produces with John Lucas. The video poems bring poetry off the static page and into cinematic motion. *Citizen* engages multiple genres simultaneously, while also capturing the reader with its address to "you." *Just Us* (2020) builds upon the aim of inviting public conversation, shifting from "An American Lyric" to "An American Conversation" while incorporating an even wider array of visual and collaged materials, including facsimile pages from Thomas Jefferson's *Notes on the State of Virginia*.

Rankine's poems are printed in multiple anthologies, including *Great American Prose Poems: From Poe to the Present* (2003), *Best American Poetry* (2001), and *The Garden*

Thrives: Twentieth Century African-American Poetry (1996) ("Claudia Rankine"). In addition, Rankine is the editor of several anthologies including *American Poets in the 21st Century: Poetics of Social Engagement*, with co-editor Michael Dowdy (Wesleyan UP 2018), *The Racial Imaginary: Writers on Race in the Life of the Mind* with Beth Loffreda and Max Cap King (Fence Books 2015), *Eleven More American Women Poets in the 21st Century: Poetics Across North America*, with co-editor Lisa Sewell (Wesleyan UP 2012), *American Poets in the 21st Century: The New Poetics*, also with co-editor Lisa Sewell (Wesleyan UP 2007), and *American Women Poets in the 21st Century: Where Lyric Meets Language*, with co-editor Juliana Spahr (Wesleyan UP 2002).

Rankine is also the founder of the *Open Letter Project: Race and the Creative Imagination.* In "An Open Letter from Claudia Rankine," she invites "discussion about the creative imagination, creative writing and race," asking readers to submit one to five pages responding to questions such as: "If you write about race frequently what issues, difficulties, advantages, and disadvantages do you negotiate?" and "If fear is a component of your reluctance to approach this subject could you examine that in a short essay that would be made public?" (Spears). This project, initiated by a keynote address that Rankine gave at the Association of Writers and Writing Programs (AWP) conference in 2016, furthers her aim of encouraging public discussions of writing and race. In 2023, the AWP states that the organization's mission is to amplify "the voices of writers and the academic programs and organizations that serve them while championing diversity and excellence in creative writing," with one of their four "strategic objectives" being to respond "with reenergized support for our increasingly diverse membership that has been and is changing our association for the better" (*AWP*). Rankine is an influential voice across platforms, including the AWP.

She is also the author of several plays: *Provenance of Beauty: A South Bronx Travelogue*; *Existing Conditions*, co-authored with Casey Llewellyn; *The White Card* (Graywolf 2019) which premiered in February 2018; and *HELP*, which opened in previews in March of 2020 at The Shed in New York City but closed due to the COVID-19 pandemic. Commissioned by New York City's Foundry Theatre, *Provenance of Beauty*, a poetic travelogue created with Melanie Joseph, was performed in September–October 2009 on a bus touring the South Bronx, and revived in 2011 at Arena Stage in Washington, D.C. A *New York Times* theatre critic describes the experience of the bus tour as follows:

> You board on 121st Street in East Harlem, donning headsets attached to small radio receivers. As the bus crosses the Willis Avenue Bridge and winds its way through the South Bronx, three narrators — two recorded and one live, sitting in the front — provide poetic commentary and factual context for the sights you see through the windows, making the complex history of a rarely celebrated neighborhood take root in your heart and mind. (Isherwood)

The play achieves a multi-vocality also present in Rankine's other works that do not rely on a single voice. Frank Scheck— who notes that the sites on the bus tour include "a Con Ed substation hidden behind a façade of fake town houses; The Point Cultural Center and its famous graffiti murals; and Barretto Point Park, which is right between a sewage treatment plant and a floating prison barge"—calls the play "informative, poetic, provocative, entertaining and, finally, haunting" (Scheck). *The Provenance of Beauty* was a 2011 Distinguished Development Project Selection in the American Voices New Play Institute at Arena Stage and was also nominated for a Drama Desk Award (S. Bell). *Existing Conditions*, a three-act play, was commissioned by the Mellon Foundation and Haverford College; act one was performed at Haverford in April 2010. Rankine's other collaboration with Llewellyn, "Theatre of Intimacy and Abandon," appears in *Imagined Theatres: Writing for a Theoretical Stage*, edited by Daniel Sack.

The White Card opened on February 28, 2018, at the Emerson Paramount Center on the Robert J. Orchard Stage in Boston, in collaboration with ArtsEmerson and the American Repertory Theatre. It is the first of her plays to be published. For Rankine, *The White Card* organically followed the book *Citizen* and the conversations she had with audiences while on her book tour. She explains: "I wanted to write *The White Card* because it seemed to me that people had a difficult time talking about race. And I thought, 'What would it look like?' which is why I wanted it to be in the theater. And if my work can be a conduit that you can have the conversation through then I'm honored by that" ("Claudia Rankine on Being a Conduit for Conversation"). *The White Card* takes place in the Manhattan loft of a wealthy developer, Charles, and his wife, Virginia, private art collectors, both of whom are white, and who fancy themselves as supporters of diverse artists. In a send-up of "Guess Who's Coming to Dinner?" Charles and Virginia are hosting a dinner party for up-and-coming artist, Charlotte, a Black woman whose artwork they wish to purchase. The other guests are their calculating art dealer and their son, an outspoken racial justice activist and student at Columbia University. These characters are also white, making Charlotte the single Black character.

The play addresses contemporary issues including cultural appropriation and ownership, and the ethics of viewing Black death as spectacle, a problem heightened in our social media age. The tensions at the dinner table continue to rise throughout the first scene, at times also raising the audience's anxiety, as responses to cringe-inducing racist and sexist comments make their way into the characters' table talk. Yet Rankine views the discomfort that the play provokes as providing opportunities for needed discussion: "The scenes in this one-act play, for all the characters' disagreements, stalemates, and seeming impasses, explore what happens if one is willing to stay in the room when it is painful to bear the pressure to listen and the obligation to respond" (*The White Card | Graywolf Press*). Staying together in the room is key here, rather than avoiding issues that are particularly difficult, both emotionally and intellectually, to discuss. Rankine stresses the importance of putting people together in physical space, which the experience of viewing live theatre productions enables. "Theater is not passively being able to take what you want and leave the rest. Theater involves taking from one body into another. That's how I got from *Citizen* to *The White Card*, from the page to the theater" (Dolen). There is also a staged adaptation of *Citizen*, called *Citizen Affirmed*. Emphasizing the importance of encounter, *Citizen Affirmed* has been performed with audiences seated on two sides of the aisle facing one another, rather than the stage.

The world premiere of *Help* took place at The Shed in New York City in March 2022. Rankine published an essay in *The New York Times Magazine* (July 2019) called "I Wanted to Know What White Men Thought About Their Privilege. So I Asked," which received 2,197 online comments. "The text spoken by white people in the piece was primarily culled from responses to the *Times* article," as well as "public statements by men and women in the government and public life and interviews conducted with white men by civil rights activist and theologian Ruby Sales," filmmaker Whitney Dow, or Rankine ("Claudia Rankine on Writing *Help*"). The main character of *Help*, named only the "Narrator," is a Black woman who recounts these "real-life conversations with white people that take place in transitional spaces like airports. As the stories unfold through monologues and staged scenarios, *Help* explores how these conversations can go right, wrong, or raise new questions about our fragile democracy" ("Help"). Rankine explains that this play was influenced by the writing of Fred Moten, Saidiya Hartman, Lauren Berlant, Frank Wilderson III, Jared Sexton, and Christina Sharpe ("Help").

Rankine also produces multi-media projects in collaboration with her husband, documentary photographer and filmmaker John Lucas, including the video series "The Situation," available at various sites online. As noted above, Rankine's poem scripts for the videos also appear in *Citizen*. Reporter Felicia R. Lee explains: "Some of the words in 'Citizen' were written as scripts to accompany videos on topics ranging from Hurricane Katrina to the World Cup" that the couple produced together (Lee). Rankine explains that the collaboration fruitfully draws on their individual talents; she stresses language, while Lucas thinks visually. In "Situation One," a video from a now infamous encounter during the 2006 FIFA World Cup Final plays in slow motion while Rankine reads from a poem text. In the video, Italian player Marco Materazzi taunts Zindine Zidane from the French team and Zidane eventually turns and headbutts Materazzi in the chest, knocking him to the ground.

While some said the insults were directed toward Zidane's mother or sister, the text includes repetition of insults Materazzi also possibly directed toward Zidane concerning his Arab and Algerian heritage that recall France's 132-year colonial occupation of Algeria, and the concomitant penetration of racist attitudes about Algerians, Muslims, and Arabs into French public discourse. Despite Zidane's superstar status, "Situation One" reveals that some still consider him an outsider because of his Arab heritage, his religion, and financially impoverished childhood in Marseille's infamous "La Castellane" suburban housing estate. The video poem thus relates: "The Algerian men for their part are a target of criticism for their European comrades. Arise directly to the level of tragedy" (Lucas). "Situation One" is a significant example of addressing race outside of a U.S.-centric point of view.

"Situation 5," features Black men riding alone in cars, quietly gazing out rainy windows. The text Rankine reads in the video poem, which varies at points from the script for "February 26, 2012 / In Memory of Trayvon Martin," printed in *Citizen* (Rankine, *Citizen* 88-91), begins as follows: "My brothers are notorious. Though they have never been to prison, they are imprisoned" and goes on to note that "the hearts of my brothers are broken" (Rankine and Lucas, "Situation 5"). Toward the middle of the 4 minute, 32 second video, a quick series of still images from Jim Crow America appear on the right side of the screen, including a picture of Emmett Till, a "help wanted" sign that states "whites only," and a scene from a lynching. Additional historical images are incorporated, including video footage of LAPD officers beating Black motorist Rodney King even as he lay on the ground.

Another poem script, "Stop-and-Frisk," begins with the following situation:

> I knew whatever was in front of me was happening and then
> the police vehicle came to a screeching halt in front of me
> like they were setting up a blockade. Everywhere were
> flashes, a siren sounding and a stretched-out roar. Get on the
> ground. Get on the ground now. Then I just knew (*Citizen* 105).

One of the phrases repeated in the poem script, "And you were not the guy yet still you fit the description because there is only one guy who is always the guy fitting the description," (108, 109) emphasizes that African Americans and Latinos as a group, as well as individual Black and Latinx men, are repeatedly assumed to be "the guy fitting the description."

In the "Stop-and-Frisk" video poem, a pair of young Black men enter a sneaker and clothing boutique. Two other young Black men are already shopping in the store. They are smiling as they interact with one another and try on clothes. This scene would remain pleasant, though unremarkable, if not for the soundtrack and the images projected onto the men. Reflected in the glass window of the store, as if a police car with flashing lights is pointed toward the store's front, the viewer sees a number of lights flashing simultaneously: a flashing blue and white siren, as well as flashing yellow lights (Lucas, "Claudia Rankine's Poem 'Stop and Frisk'").

The effect is disturbing and obscures the entire frame of the young men enjoying one another's company. The lights demonstrate that Black men are under surveillance even as they are going about their daily lives, doing ordinary things. In one of the looping soundtracks played simultaneously with Rankine's recitation of the poem, two voices repeat: "You don't know why? I don't know why" (Lucas, "Claudia Rankine's Poem 'Stop and Frisk'"). These questions echo those from the poem script: "Then why are you pulling me over? Why am I pulled over?" (106). Such questions are posed again and again in personal cell phone videos, often shared on social media platforms, of police detaining Black citizens without cause.

Rankine and Lucas have also collaborated on art installations such as "Stamped" and "whiteness, inc." In "Stamped," which investigates the relationship between blondness and whiteness, "[t]he artists take a dual approach to their subject: photographs and videos of blond hair, sometimes printed on stamps, and audio snippets of Ms. Rankine asking people about their fair hair" (Schwendener et al.). "whiteness, inc.," published in *Artforum* in 2016, presents photographs with collaged texts from advertisements to explore the relationship between whiteness and consumer capitalism (Rankine and Lucas, "Whiteness, Inc.").

Rankine has had a long career as a professor of creative writing and has held faculty positions at Case Western Reserve

University (1994-1996), Barnard College (1996–2003), University of Georgia (2003-2004), University of Houston (2004-2006), Pomona College (2006–2016), and the University of Southern California (2015–2016), where she held the Aerol Arnold Chair of English, prior to joining the faculty of Yale University as the Frederick Iseman Professor of Poetry in the Departments of English and African American Studies. She left her position at Yale at the end of 2020-2021 academic year to join the creative writing faculty at New York University, beginning in Fall 2021. The move reflects Rankine's growing investment in playwriting and production. She notes: "I find myself involved more and more in theater in New York. So the decision to take the NYU position will allow me to teach and attend rehearsals and write in a more fluid way" (Hahamy and Tian). Rankine has taught at several other colleges and universities as well, including the Queens College MFA Program for Writers, the Iowa Writers' Workshop, the Warren Wilson College MFA Program for Writers, and Cleveland State University. Rankine and Lucas have a daughter, Ula Lucas.

This book provides the first scholarly introduction to Rankine's poetry, with chapters on *Nothing in Nature Is Private* (Cleveland State University 1994), *The End of the Alphabet* (Grove Press 1998), *PLOT* (Grove Press 2001), *Don't Let Me Be Lonely: An American Lyric* (Graywolf Press 2004), and *Citizen: An American Lyric* (Graywolf Press 2014). Just as Rankine's writing reaches across form and genre, each book seeks connection from among seemingly disparate, or estranged, categories: African Americans and nature, language and silence, pregnant women and their own unrecognizable bodies. The later books instruct the reader in ways to recognize connections that are already there, but unspoken or unrecognized: a heightened attention to "terrorists" and nationalism, advertising and depression, television and loneliness, and seeming "slights" of interpersonal racism with the dangers of structural racism that can cut short a life. Rankine is an essential poet for the twentieth and twenty-first century, whose collaborations in visual art and video, as well as her work as a playwright, expand her ability to reach audiences with new forms of reading and seeing that can lead to constructing new forms of relationality.

For additional biographical information see:

Academy of American Poets / poets.org
https://poets.org/poet/claudia-rankine

Blue Flower Arts
https://blueflowerarts.com/artist/claudia-rankine/

Encyclopedia Britannica
https://www.britannica.com/biography/Claudia-Rankine

MacArthur Foundation
https://www.macfound.org/fellows/967/

The Poetry Foundation
https://www.poetryfoundation.org/poets/claudia-rankine

1

Before *Citizen*: Lyric Subjectivity and the Language of Experience in Claudia Rankine's *Nothing in Nature is Private*

Published twenty years before her best-selling and multiple award-winning book, *Citizen: An American Lyric,* Claudia Rankine's first book, *Nothing in Nature Is Private* (Cleveland State University 1994), won the 1993 Cleveland State University Poetry Center's International Poetry Competition. On the publication of Rankine's first poetry collection, Robert Haas, former Poet Laureate of the United States and Distinguished Professor in Poetry and Poetics at the University of California, Berkeley, called Rankine a "fiercely gifted young poet" ("Cover copy"). Mervyn Morris, poet and professor emeritus at the University of the West Indies, Mona, Jamaica, notes that she "represents brilliantly the prismatic vision of a Jamaican, middle class, intellectual black woman living in America" ("Cover copy," suggesting that the vantage point from which to read *Nothing in Nature is Private* is one based on the author's racial, gendered, class-based, and immigrant identities).

Jamaican-born poets, including Rankine, "who carry the double identity as Caribbean and African Americans," Derrilyn E. Morrison argues, "give evidence that the Caribbean discourse of identity is shifting gears, moving beyond the boundaries of traditional cultural communities as poets explore their current standing in relation to the wider diaspora" (5). Thus, Morrison argues, these Caribbean poets are "shifting identity politics as they create works that engage in the task of revising history and re-inscribing the black community as a speaking, subjective presence within the body politic" (6). Revising the historical relationships of African American and Afro-Caribbean poets to this body politic, *Nothing in Nature is Private* thus interrogates something broader than the individual: the formation of national identity. In fact, from the title of the first poem, "American Light," in her first book, to the subtitle of her two recent books of poetry ("An American Lyric") Rankine has dwelt in the history and multiple meanings of the "American."

Rankine, however, claims to have forgotten her first book, a not uncommon disavowal also expressed by other accomplished poets. (French poet Danielle Collobert is said to have hunted down and destroyed all the copies of her first book.) Yet, despite Rankine's claim, *Nothing in Nature is Private* lays out important investigations that continue to be foundational to her writing practice, which allow readers to consider deeply a Black female subject not in isolation or primarily through interiority (what Stephanie Burt calls "a more or less introspective, meditative individual" in a lyric poem, 423) but a subject constructed relationally with the American landscape, history of the Americas, and literary lineages. Such an analysis enlarges debates both about how subjectivity is framed and how it is related to poetic form.

In an interview conducted in 2006, at which point Rankine had done a great deal of thinking about form in her then four published books of poems, Rankine explains: "Form has everything to do with content. We know this from Olson. I love the potential openness of the page–there is so much unspoken 'underneath-ness' in language. I try to use the page to illustrate the mind's meanderings–to suggest silence, for example, and to represent all the ways the subject is approached in my own mind" (Rankine, "Poetry Daily Prose Feature: Interview with Claudia Rankine"). Poet Charles Olson, author of "Projective Verse" rejected so-called "academic" verse, "with its closed forms and alleged artifice" (Olson, "Projective Verse") and argues instead for what he describes as "the possibilities of the breath," as well as "what can also be called COMPOSITION BY FIELD, as opposed to inherited line, stanza, over-all form" (Olson, "Projective Verse"). Olson asserts that "FORM IS NEVER MORE THAN AN EXTENSION OF CONTENT" (Olson, "Projective Verse"). Olson shows how each poem's form emerges from the necessities imposed by breathe, kinetics, and other physical processes, rather than starting from a pre-determined form. Such a process made the typewriter essential for his process, given that it can "indicate exactly the breath, the pauses, the suspensions even of syllables, the juxtapositions even of parts of phrases, which [the poet] intends" (Olson, "Projective Verse"). In drawing from Olson, Rankine re-embodies Black subjectivity, expanding the possibilities of lyric presence.

However, as interviewers Jennifer Flescher and Robert N. Caspar note, "You've said that in *Nothing in Nature Is Private* the subject did not determine the form," and they ask her how her ideas about form have been revised (Rankine, "Poetry Daily Prose Feature: Interview with Claudia Rankine"). Rankine explains, "That book [*Nothing in Nature Is Private*] came out of an MFA program, where I behaved a bit like a tennis player—trying to hit poems over the net back to a roomful of people. There's that constant struggle between satisfying the expectations of the program and what your unconscious wants to investigate" (Rankine, "Poetry Daily Prose Feature: Interview with Claudia Rankine"). Seeing the workshop experience as a competitive sport is a telling revelation. While Rankine acknowledges the importance of the guidance that she received at Columbia University, she also addresses some of the problems that the MFA system may create: "The danger with MFA programs is they create a sort of factory: at the end of day seven or year three, you're going to complete something. So you strive toward that completion, and you're not encouraged toward messiness" (Rankine, "Poetry Daily Prose Feature: Interview with Claudia Rankine"). Indeed, the neat form of the poems in her first book do not reflect the kind of "messiness" and resistance to closure that we will see in her later work.

In another interview (published by Verse Press in 2005) Rankine describes her desire to depart from her early poems' emphases upon what she calls "typecasting" her early life experiences, which had become "a performance of blackness and immigration." That is, she had begun to recreate in her writing the experiences audiences expected to hear from a Black, immigrant poet, which caused the poems to engender forms of stereotype or inauthenticity. These poems enact a false sense of closure that became insufficient for Rankine because, "The poems began to enact a pre-conceived condition," pre-determined conclusions about what a Black, immigrant, woman poet should sound like (Rankine, "Claudia Rankine" 147). Certainly, her next book, *The End of the Alphabet*, published in 1998, places her in conversation with Language Writers, including Lyn Hejinian, who explore subjectivities through formally experimental processes that move outside of a unitary lyric subject, linearity, and presumably transparent language.

Yet, there are multiple ways to consider how subjectivity and experience can be read in *Nothing in Nature is Private*. Paula M. L. Moya presents one possible approach, in arguing that experience is both epistemically and politically significant. In contrast to Judith Butler's assertion in the influential work *Gender Trouble*, which asserts that "selves (and the subjectivities through which they come into being) [have] no existence apart from the discourses that produce them" (Moya 9), or Michel Foucault, who in "Concern for Truth" explores the relationship between thought and truth "in order to weaken the hegemonic power of our present-day truths by revealing them as discursively constructed and historically contingent" (Moya 10). Moya puts more emphasis on what she calls "verifiable aspects of the social world"; she argues for the importance of "subjective" experience—not just discursive identity formation.

Moya writes, "I understand identities to be socially significant and context-specific ideological constructs that nevertheless refer in non-arbitrary (if partial) ways to verifiable aspects of the social world. Moreover, I contend that it is precisely because identities have a referential relationship to the world that they are politically and epistemically important" (13). Butler, Foucault, and others stress that the discursive nature of identity construction necessarily unsettles any reliance upon the apparent transparency of language, and that what Butler calls formerly "culturally unintelligible and impossible" selves that already exist will be possible only when we are able to expose and understand the constructedness of those selves (149). Moya's work enrichens this analysis by stressing the connections between discursive *and* sociopolitical contexts: "identities instantiate the links between individuals and groups and central organizing principles of our society. Consequently, an examination of individual identities can provide important insights about fundamental aspects of U.S. society" (13), an examination which Rankine's early poems enact on the page, constructing a new identity in a traditional form.

This is evident in her choices concerning form in *Nothing in Nature is Private*, for example, transforming the pastoral form into a Black pastoral, similar to the mode of Claude McKay's Shakespearean sonnets, which become containers for expressing Black revolutionary resistance, rather than examination of "timeless" concerns, such as love, beauty, or time. Camille T. Dungy notes that "Black Nature" writing necessarily holds contradictory experiences. For Black poets, Dungy argues, meditations upon trees (particularly trees in the American South) can lead to "a history steeped in often arbitrarily brutal and always dehumanizing racism" *and* "a renewed connection to the natural world," thus complicating the tradition of the pastoral that portrays often idealized visions of nature as "diversion" and a "construction of a culture that dreams, through landscape and animal life, of a certain luxury or innocence" (xxi). Rankine's employment of a Black pastoral deepens and complicates the history of the pastoral, while also introducing content that challenges the lyric's putative connection to timeless individuality.

Although the definition of lyric often places the form in opposition to narrative, as M. H. Abrams describes "lyric" in his *Glossary of Literary Terms*, "any fairly short, non-narrative poem presenting a single speaker who expresses a state of mind or a process of thought and feeling," the conventional workshop poems that Rankine was writing at the beginning of her publishing career often rely upon short narratives or story-telling, though their primary form is lyric (Abrams 108). Critical race theory's important contribution to understanding how narrative can be a means through which to disrupt hegemonic legal and political discourse thickens this analysis of genre. Critical race theory pioneer Richard Delgado explains: "Stories, parables, chronicles, and narratives, are powerful means for destroying mindset—the bundle of presuppositions, received wisdoms, and shared understandings against a background of which legal and political discourse takes place" (2413). Critical race theory, developed by legal scholars, exposes how the law and other systems, intended to be neutral, can actually reinforce inequality in their enforcement. In confronting the conception of "Americanness," the poems in *Nothing in Nature is Private* push against typical discourses of nation, as represented in American landscape, history, and literature, and the power they represent.

Nothing in Nature is Private contains 24 poems, separated into five sections. All of the poems are left justified, with an occasional indented line, and (unlike much of Rankine's later experiments with the fragment and parataxis, use of the white space of the page, and with the prose poem) are conventionally lineated. The poem, "American Light," is alone, making up the entirety of section one. It begins with a pastoral image of a pair of cardinals, coupled with a description of the sky's reflection in a puddle of water:

Cardinals land
on a branch, female and male.
The sky shivers
in puddles created of night rain. (Rankine 2)

Although the "shiver" of the sky may suggest more disconcerting, the reader can also easily picture images that waver in pools of water, both large and small. In addition, the speaker immediately assuages any potential discomfort associated with shivering in darkness with the visual pleasure of pastoral beauty, as "Speckled particles dance / in a path of light" (2). Yet, surrounded by this natural beauty, the poet quickly brings the reader back to a more difficult reality.

Even though "it seems / it doesn't matter what's in the road," we are reminded at once of what it means to consider the *American* world of light and dark: "Then the shadow of a black oak / leans forward like a wounded man" (2). Significantly, the image of the tree is also an allusion to Paul Laurence Dunbar's poem, "The Haunted Oak," a poem about lynching in which the anthropomorphic tree exudes the pain of the murder victim: "I feel the rope against my bark, / And the weight of him in my grain," the speaker/oak reveals, "I feel in the throe of his final woe / The touch of my own last pain" (Dunbar, "The Haunted Oak"). Thus, as Angela Hume concludes, Rankine "explicitly realigns her pastoral inheritance from the Romantic tradition to that of what we might call a black pastoral tradition—one according to which nature is always implicated in histories of racial violence" (Hume 96), examples of which are contained throughout the anthology *Black Nature: Four Centuries of African American Nature Poetry* (2009).

This pain radiates throughout history, for the shadow of the black oak that appears in the first stanza of Rankine's poem is also "on ships," and "in fields / for years, for centuries even, in heat / colored by strokes of red" (2). Here are the contradictions of the American landscape: the brilliant red of the male cardinal in the pastoral is also the red of the blood that has been shed into and for this land and the creation of this nation. Beauty and danger radiate from the same source and the speaker insists that we view both. The same light that "makes clouds iridescent / islands in the sky" also "insists on a shadow in the road" (3). From the moment we are confronted with the shadow of the black oak, we are also confronted with America's wounds: the wounds of slavery, the wounds of lynching, the continuing wounds of race that reverberate into the twentieth century—what Saidya Hartman calls "the afterlife of slavery" (Hartman 4).

For this "lit landscape" of America conceives a shadow of a face that is "dark, wide-open" with eyes that are "bloodshot / from what had come before" (2). The wounds of history remain in the "peeled / back places" of the lit landscape, "making the place uncomfortable" (2). Yet, crucially, there is "no fault / in the self" that is the landscape's shadow, a shadow that also contains "a gesture of wanting, coveting / the American light" (2). The poem prompts us to consider who is bathed in American light, warmed by its presence, and who is cast in shadow. Offering an answer to these questions, the speaker reveals a moment in which she experiences self-recognition within the shadow: "I realize I recognize myself." The speaker takes a step further as the poem develops, owning the shadow, as one must own historical facts: "I step into my shadow / as if not to take it anymore, / and wonder where I am going" (3). When the speaker claims her space in the shadow of American history, while simultaneously refusing to accept the subjugation prescribed to it, she has claimed a new subject position. Unsettling her presumed place in history, it is no longer clear what road she should follow.

Stepping into the shadow, as if into American history, the speaker doesn't want "any trouble," yet she notes the danger in this beautiful place:

> . . . but when the sun
> goes down on this aged,
> dirt road, will I end
> in dark woods, or make it home? (3)

The question at the end of this stanza, which also ends the poem, is multiple in its meanings. Will the speaker die in the dark woods as "the sun / goes down on this aged, / dirt road," or will she make it home safely (3)? Will she stay in the darkness and make the "sweet sad shadow, sun charred / on the open road" her home? Or, refusing to "take it anymore" can she step into and claim the American light?

The epigraph to *Nothing in Nature is Private* offers answers to these questions by claiming a literary lineage. The quotation is a selection from fellow Caribbean author, Martinican poet and statesman, Aimé Césaire's well-known *Cahier d'un retour au pays natal* (*Notebook of a Return to My Native Land*), the first version of which was published in 1939. *Notebook* explores many of the same dilemmas that Rankine confronts in regard to landscape, history, and lineage. The quote from Césaire states, in part:

> I would go to this land of mine and say to it:
> "Embrace me without fear . . . And if all I can do is speak, it is
> for you I shall speak."
> And again I would say:
> "My mouth shall be the mouth of those calamities that have no
> mouth, my voice the freedom of those who break down in the
> solitary confinement of despair." (xi)

Given Rankine's concerns with landscape, it is critical that the speaker of Césaire's poem addresses the land itself. The land here, like the land in Rankine's opening poem, contains within it the history of "calamities" and "despair." Yet the poet's task that Césaire and Rankine take on is to be both the voice of that suffering *and* the voice of freedom. Rankine accomplishes this in part by toggling back and forth between the pastoral and bits of historical narrative—showing how the same images can be used to reveal despair and liberation.

Moreover, in these early poems, Rankine explores how to locate the self, as well as how to understand what constitutes a Black woman's body, both in its parts and as a whole, in a racialized terrain that has already prescribed meaning to her body before she was born. This is an example of lyric embodiment, a concept central to locating the lived experience of people of African descent in the Americas, rather than lyric poetry that "disembodies" and "tries to construct a new, acoustic or verbal body" (Burt 439). This embodiment is crucial precisely because the possession of self is tenuous for the Black speaker, as Rankine writes in "Descending from Darkness," a poem with an epigraph from Ralph Ellison:

> I lose hold of myself
> my place,
> my exact presence.

Everywhere it is dark. (50)

The speaker attempts "to see past / slaves-- / who were a people" yet, they hand her "a lineage of pain" (51). It is necessary to stress that "slaves" "were a people," not a noun (slave) that replaces their personage, but enslaved *persons*.

32

Say only: Once
there was this: slave ships,
lynching.

Then I am injured. (54)

Revealing the history of injury, the speaker considers her own face repeatedly and discovers this traumatic history in her own reflection: "tracked in my face / is what must be faced" (52). It is the face of her mother; it is the face of her ancestors. Given the history that her own face reflects back to her, she must develop a new anatomy: "My sense of myself includes / an organ for darkness" (50). The "organ" is not only racial embodiment, but the "darkness" of racialized violence.

Self-identification and place are central to this work. The poet's literal place changes—from the Jamaica of young childhood to the U.S.—creating moments of association and dislocation that are explored in the poems. This is what Morrison calls "the outsider/insider perspectives embraced by Caribbean transnationals" that "allow them to retain strong cultural ties to the Caribbean, which are reflected or inflected in their writing," a description applicable to Rankine's first book (6). The dislocation is at times so laden with trauma that the body disintegrates into its parts, as in "Landscape at Dawn":

Within
you locate all defined parts of yourself,
        the lungs,
        the brain,
        the heart,
        and so on,
to place on rocks like markers to exist (72)

Although the "you" addressed in the poem knows "most intimately / this landscape" she remains unsteady because she feels it disowns her (73). All history is present—not past—and one cannot feel connected to oneself or the land, even in the landscape at dawn. Thus, "each step taken / becomes all bruised time / in the overdone spring" and "another start to a dubious end" (73) as the speaker tries to identify her "parts" in order to confirm her own existence.

Furthermore, in the epigraph Rankine selected for her first book, Césaire writes:

And on the way I would say to myself:
"And more than anything, my body, as well as my soul beware of assuming the sterile attitude of a spectator, for life is not a spectacle, a sea of miseries is not a proscenium, a man screaming is not a dancing bear . . ." (xi)

This epigraph seems particularly pertinent for a book that Rankine describes as a product of an MFA program in which she was competing with both the workshop audience and the program's expectations. How can a young Black poet write about race for a workshop in a way that will not reduce the experiences of people of color to spectacle? Moreover, how should a poet position her own perspective in order to avoid "assuming the sterile attitude of a spectator"? Rankine, therefore, begins with a deep investment in the ethics of representation, an investment that will stay with her, as a version of this same Césaire quote is used later as an epigraph to *Don't Let Me Be Lonely*.

Certainly, she is wrestling with these questions concerning representation and perspective in "In Transit," a ten-page poem in section two of *Nothing in Nature is Private*. "In Transit" explores both being looked at, and what it means to look. While "In Transit" is perhaps most productively read as a set of interrelated poems on the same theme, the long poem does show Rankine already considering poetic form beyond the individual, often one-page, contained lyric. "Transit" here refers to traffic, motion, the changing and unchanged. While some sections of the poem are set in interior spaces, most take place on the street, or as the first stanza tells us, "in the neighborhood" (9). Each section confronts incidents of violence.

For example, a lover for whose safety the Black female speaker fears finally admits that he was cut off in traffic while riding his bike home from the gym by a "frat- / boy-type" who yells *"why / don't you take your black ass back to Africa?"* (13). He whispers his admission into her ear, a closely held secret. In another scene, a black couple is surrounded by "a sea of black youths" who cry: *"Well. Well. What have / we here, bourgie blacks in living color"* (16), and in another vignette, a woman is confronted by a man who sets a kitchen knife up against her cheek. Against these scenes of violence, the speaker yearns to feel comfort in the presence of Black men: "Who I want to see / is my brother in the face of the man who was / walking and now stands close" yet "The kitchen knife he holds demands / everything" (17). The speaker, throughout this poem and throughout the book, attempts to make sense of her contradictory positions within difficult and ordinary occurrences in American life. Rankine does not provide easy answers about race and gender for her readers, who must contemplate these questions for themselves.

In the perpetual motion of the neighborhood even in "broadest daylight," the speaker relates: "the complexion I'll know all my life" is "the complexion of my fear" (9). As a Black person in the United States, she worries for her safety and integrity while conducting the daily business of life. For example, on the opening page of this section, the speaker is followed down the street and is afraid for both herself and her brother (who could be a biological or familial brother, or a figure metaphorically standing in for Black men as a whole), "his body, / a pulsing stick figure / to be shot down or etched into a cell wall" (9). In contrast to the motion of the street, the brother is immobilized by violence.

His body is reduced to a stick figure that is either killed or imprisoned.

In the next section, police club a Black man, who the speaker is clear to emphasize "is altogether a different thing" than a generic "man" who readers presume to be white. The speaker, in terror, must know who the downed man is: *"Do I know this man? / Do I recognize his body?"* (10). The speaker is "a mother, / brother, sister, wife running red / lights past breathless asphalt" (10). The "I" who runs red lights to get to the man being beaten by police encompasses all those intimately related to Black men.

Rankine emphasizes the way in which readers are trained automatically to assume that a "man" is white, unless his race is specifically identified, while also demonstrating that people of color are often the only literary characters who are specifically racialized, when she writes:

Passing, what I heard
was the man asking,
the white man asking,
(as if he, the other
were going nowhere)
the white man asking
for a minute
of the other's time. (11)

The speaker goes on to describe a scene in which the white man has accidentally locked his keys in the car and is wondering,

if he, the other, could,
perhaps, get in, could,
somehow, please, break
in and get, please,
the keys out of the car. (11)

A number of assumptions, in addition to the reader's built-in assumptions about race, are tested here. The white man seems to presume that the "the other," the Black man, has nowhere to go and can be bothered with his unusual request. The white man also must presume that, unlike himself, a Black man must know how to break into a car.

Moreover, after taking in this scene, the reader's eyes immediately are drawn back to the facing page where the police are:

> clubbing the man's head, his chest,
> while the man, rather, the black man
> (who is altogether a different thing)
>
> is losing on the pavement. (10)

Now the reader must consider: Are the police clubbing the man after having presumed that he was breaking into a car and trying to steal it, when actually he is trying to fulfill the white man's request to retrieve his keys? Making this connection produces a nauseating shock in the reader that causes her to consider more deeply the breathless terror of the family members represented on the page.

Of course, the man on the pavement in this section could also be an allusion to Rodney King, who members of the LAPD viciously kicked, tased, and beat with batons even as he lay on the ground following a traffic chase in 1991. The *Los Angeles Times* reported that his injuries included a fractured cheekbone, 11 broken bones at the base of his skull, and a broken leg, and King subsequently suffered the effects of permanent brain damage. This catastrophe gained national attention because a man awakened by noise of the late night incident, 31-year-old plumber and Argentinian immigrant George Holliday, videotaped it from his apartment balcony and thereafter attempted to get the police, and then the media, to take note of what he had seen and recorded (Ortiz).

In 2006, Holliday noted that he was still astounded by what he saw: "I was thinking, 'What did the guy do to deserve this beating?' I came from a different culture, where people would get disappeared with no due process. Police would pick people up on suspicion. I didn't expect this in the U.S." (Goldstein). In an interview with NPR's Karen Grigsby Bates, lawyer and civil rights activist Connie Rice describes how the LAPD's "aggressive paramilitary policing" combined with "a culture that was mean and cruel, racist and abusive of force in communities of color, particularly poor communities of color" created a police presence akin to "an occupying force" in Los Angeles during that time (Sastry and Grigsby Bates).

Thus, on the day in April 1992 when the jury acquitted the four LAPD officers indicted for beating King, the city of Los Angeles—already simmering in racial and economic turmoil and tension with the police—boiled over in a six-day uprising. The videotape of the officers beating King had been widely viewed on the news, "And yet, we saw a verdict that told us we couldn't trust our lying eyes. That what we thought was open and shut was really 'a reasonable expression of police control' toward a black motorist," explains University of Southern California criminal justice and law professor Jody David Armour, "When the verdict came out, it was a stunner for people coast to coast. My jaw dropped" (Sastry and Grigsby Bates).

Police response to the violence following the verdict was slow, and in some cases non-existent. "That night, [LA Chief of Police] Gates went to speak at a fundraiser in West Los Angeles and reportedly ordered cops to retreat. Police did not respond to incidents of looting and violence around the city until almost three hours after the original rioting broke out" (Sastry and Grigsby Bates). During this time of police inaction, white truck driver Reginald Denny, who knew nothing about the riots, drove through the intersection of Florence and Normandie where he was pulled from his truck and viciously beaten by rioters, as news helicopters broadcast the violence live, a scene documented in the poem: *"This—can you believe it—this is live. / Live!* As the white man was beaten by / the blow-for-blow circle of black men" (Rankine 14). Like King, Denny suffered vicious blows to the head, resulting in multiple skull fractures and permanent brain damage. "The white man, pulled from his truck, / had done nothing, and still so much time / to understand" (14). Here, lyric meets narrative, and private emotion connects with public events.

Four African American residents of South Central— Bobby Green, Lei Yuille, Titus Murphy and Terri Barnett—who had seen the attack on television, sped to Denny's aid. "Despite the risk to their own lives, they grabbed Denny, put him back into his cab and drove him to a nearby hospital where doctors were able to save his life" ("The L.A. Riots"). Barnett remembers watching the cops drive right by rioters without stopping. "There were four cops in each car that passed by," Barnett told NPR in 1992, "They saw us. They looked right through us" (Sastry and Grigsby Bates). The beatings of King as well as Denny, and the taping and broadcast of these events, are central to issues that will continue to circulate in Rankine's writing. *Citizen* contains a continually updated list in each edition of unarmed African Americans killed by the police. *Don't Let Me Be Lonely* contains images of television screens, illustrating Rankine's continuing investigation of media and representation. Rankine and husband John Lucas have produced their own video "situations" that accompany Rankine's poems. Her work asks: What are the differences between seeing and witnessing? What does it mean when two people view the same event and come away with radically different interpretations of what constitutes the truth? How are our truths informed by race and gender?

Another set of truths is investigated in the center of the book. A shift in tone is evident in this series of poems set in

Jamaica with the title "Out of Many, One," a Jamaican motto. These poems convey struggle and yearning, yet lack the persistent threat of person-on-person violence evident in the poems set in the U.S. These poems are also unique in that they employ Jamaican Patois, while the remainder of the book is written in standard English. This choice of diction roots the speakers to time and place. The section begins with a "Man called Country" walking to the beach to buy fish, moves through his migration to America, "West Indian, him left like de rest, / to sail for New York, to plant and pot / whatever fi root in de new soil" (40) and concludes with a poem called "She" in which a woman recalls her former life in Jamaica: "Daybreak, pon de continent she recall / how once she a farmer" (45). The woman remembers mango, coconut, and guava trees and "from the verandah—what she watched / since girl-time—de big belly sea" (45). The sea and the land in Jamaica are presented here as fecund and sweet, despite the many challenges people face there. This depiction of landscape contrasts greatly with the pastoral imagery of the poems set in the U.S. Though sometimes beautiful, the American landscape is not life giving. *"America go kill you"* relates the speaker in the poem "Hellshire Beach" (37).

Although this section contains a poem called "Eden" in which the woman "approached each day / with a large heart" (43), the tone is not mere nostalgia. Here Rankine again is able to portray both beauty and struggle through the prism of landscape. Sweetness is coupled with decay as "rotting mangoes melt / yellow to brown" and "them sugar / soaking the earth, / calling flies" (31). On this paradisiacal island, the land and sea are difficult taskmasters for residents who work for sustenance. For example, at the beach, fishermen are bent forward, "all of them muscle / gone tight" as they drag fish from the sea and "though the day / barely start, them tired for true" (30). Moreover, in "Back-a-Yard," Country struggles with the beautiful land: "Thirsty. Hot. The odor / of sweat at him nostrils / Country harvest greens" (31). The farmer's exhausting daily labors give rise to a dream of a better life in America, "Land full of opportunity / if you willing / to work" (36). Country believes that his willingness to work will indeed yield new opportunities if he emigrates.

In "Hellshire Beach," beauty and struggle combine once again "as cloud-- / fronds tease / moon pieces." However, as the rough grip of the wind causes the female speaker to look toward the water's edge, her perspective differs from Country's. She concludes, "*America go kill you, / but if you feel you must, / go 'long, go 'long*" (37). She mourns the loss of her husband, who is called "Country," as well as her literal country if she follows him. Like the "Out of Many, One" and "In Transit" series, many of Rankine's poems delve into such interpersonal relationships between women and men, especially Black women and Black men. These voices, and a mini script containing the characters "HE" and "SHE" in the latter series, demonstrate Rankine's assertion that, "all writing is a kind of performance," and prefigure Rankine's recent publications of drama, as well as showing her interest "in mediated responses, the media, and the clarity or lack of clarity around our own connectedness" evident in her debut collection (Rankine, "Poetry Daily Prose Feature: Interview with Claudia Rankine").

Readers also see the "privacy" of the lyric opening up to public events and the crossing of genres (lyric, narrative, dialogue) through the combination of an "embodied lyric" that challenges both of those terms. The debut collection also connects African Americans with nature, and Black people across the diaspora through the experience of immigration. This work of crossing and connection shows that *Nothing in Nature is Private* provides the foundation for what Rankine's work will become.

2

The Work of Silence in *The End of the Alphabet*

All writing is a kind of performance, but modes that fabricate closure seem less authentic to me. When I was working on *The End of the Alphabet*, for example, which was in my mind about silence, about a darkness that felt crippling, the language had to be very different from the language in something like *Don't Let Me Be Lonely*, which is interested in mediated responses, the media, and the clarity or lack of clarity around our own connectedness.

—Claudia Rankine (Rankine, "Poetry Daily Prose Feature:
Interview with Claudia Rankine
by Jennifer Flescher and Robert N. Caspar")

"Ihr das erschwiegene Wort" ("To her the word turned-to-silence")

—Paul Celan, "Argumentum e Silentio"

The End of the Alphabet, published in 1998 by Grove Press, represents a stark formal departure from Rankine's first book, *Nothing in Nature is Private* (1994), which came out of her MFA program experience. *The End of the Alphabet*'s structure disrupts conventional expectations of the individual lyric poem, with twelve sections that work together, not as individual poems that can be separated from the manuscript without losing the accrued meaning of all twelve sections. This form begins Rankine's engagement with the book-length poem, which each subsequent book also follows.

This chapter focuses on how, in *The End of the Alphabet*, Rankine writes through traumas located in the female body, including investigating how the concepts of aphasia (the inability to speak) and "hysteria" (psychological symptoms that manifest physically) are intertwined with the central concerns in the poem regarding pregnancy loss, trauma, and death. In order to develop a reading of how these subjects are approached in the poem, however, it is necessary to grapple with its central paradox: Rankine's assertion that in *The End of the Alphabet* she is writing "about silence." This paradox shapes the poem's form, language, and construction of subjectivity. There are several methods for considering how this paradox operates: Paul Celan's poetry which "... reads, and has been widely read, as a translating of silence into speech and vice versa" (Franke 140); trauma theory; and, feminist revisions of the diagnoses of "hysteria" and aphasia, which are exemplified in Gwendolyn Brooks's *Annie Allen* (1949) and the poem, "The Mother," published in 1945 in *A Street in Bronzeville*.

Rankine shows in section one of *The End of the Alphabet*, that there is no guarantee, or "assurance," that the poet can find the right words adequately to represent terrifying silence:

Assurance collapses naturally
as if each word were a dozen rare birds
flown away. And gone. (6)

Silence is organic, as the ability to give one's word or "assurance," necessarily "collapses naturally." The words themselves are also "natural," compared to a "dozen rare birds." Yet, despite the "flight" of words, the poem suggests the possibility of capturing them, as the language on the page grapples with, or points toward, the unsayable. Rankine is not the first poet to engage the subject of silence; she follows in the well-known lineage of Celan in using a poetics of silence to engage a subjectivity estranged by unspeakable wounds. She then renders that unspeakability into a form that will connect the self and the other through a shared humanness—but this is dependent on the ability to "catch" the word and return it to meaning.

The title of Celan's 1967 poetry collection, *Atemwende* (translated into English as "breathturn") is, according to one writer, "a term that the poet equates with the moment when words transcend literal meaning" ("Exhibition Catalog: Atemwende–Making").[1] "Breathturn" is also organic and embodied, as the "turn" of the breath, inhabiting the space around sounds, transforms meaning. "Catching" the word anchors it both to its meaning and to embodied experience. Rankine has a similar aim to embody, or settle into each word, which she achieves, in part, by suspending narrative to focus on individual words, so that "words were no longer markings to be skimmed over" (Rankine, "Claudia Rankine" 150). Rankine explains that "[t]he idea was that a word, any word, would cast its layers of meaning toward an emotional field that was triggered by certain unexpected juxtapositions on the page" (Rankine, "Claudia Rankine" 150–51). Casting layers of meanings creates the possibility of turning outward, and of connecting the self and Other. The ability to free the "I" from imprisoning silence is dependent upon turning outward to create an encounter or connection through the poem.

William Franke argues that Celan's poetry "suspends" language while also enabling what he describes as a step "to enter the outside world" (144):

> …when representation and even language are suspended for the moment of a turning of the breath, an "Atemwende," the poem can set the I—estranged from itself—free in its encounter with the wholly Other, who is likewise set free.

1. Ceramicist Edmund de Waal's show, *Atemwende*, at the Gagosian Gallery in New York (12 September – 19 October 2013) presents "a conversation with the poetry of Celan and de Waal's thinking about music and architecture."

> Poetry summons us to take a "step," rather than remaining purely within language, and to enter the outside world, the world outside language and representation, where otherness is encountered. (Franke 144)

Being separated from language also separates the self from representation, taking the reader to "the world outside language" which, rather than ending in stasis, opens the possibility of encountering otherness. Thus, for Celan, and likewise for Rankine, the project becomes one of freeing the "I" from the stasis of unspeakable trauma, which also enables the freeing of the "Other."

This shared freedom is created through the encounter, a touching of selves that might engender an experience of shared humanity. In his speech, "The Meridian," which he delivered upon receiving the Büchner award in 1960, Celan calls this "the mystery of the encounter," the encounter that the poem creates. "The poem is the 'connective' (*das Verbindende)*, the 'meridian,' the means of an encounter with what is wholly other, and therefore of encounter with oneself, too, as genuinely human" (Franke 139). This "encounter or "connective" is also enacted through the metaphor of a handshake: "Or Paul Celan said that the poem was no different from a handshake. *I cannot see any basic difference between a handshake and a poem*—is how Rosemary[2] Waldrop translated his German" (Rankine, *Don't Let Me Be Lonely* 130). The poem, then, reaches across time to connect disparate individuals. Rankine writes: The handshake is our decided ritual of both asserting (I am here) and handing over (here) a self to another. Hence the poem is that—Here. I am here" (Rankine, *Don't Let Me Be Lonely* 130). The poem can allow "I" and the Other to touch, to form human connection.

---

2. The correct spelling of the poet / translator's first name is Rosmarie.

Often, readers think of white space on the page as "blank," as not conveying meaning. However, the blanks, white spaces, and silences in *The End of the Alphabet* do not indicate a lack of meaning; rather, this use of silence is a literary strategy that intensifies meaning: "Although language offers no words that can articulate silence," Franke argues, "nevertheless it emerges from the failed attempt enriched by assuming a quality of pointing toward something that it cannot say, something that is killed by words" (143). The attempt to put into words a concept (silence) that no word can articulate opens up space for the ineffable, through the attempt to articulate the unsayable. As Franke suggests, Celan's poetics of silence may not point toward "a dissolving of reference," but may instead constitute "an absolute intensifying of reference in relation to history and specifically the Holocaust" (Franke 138). Indeed, though silence does not conventionally "bear sense," *The End of the Alphabet* emerges as a language that *does* convey the unspeakable in reference to historical or personal traumas. Language is "enriched" and intensified through the process of making apparent that which could not be revealed previously.

For Celan, a Romanian Jew living in France who survived the Holocaust, though his parents did not, choosing to write about the Holocaust in German renders the German language itself "the instrument of its own disembodiment" (Exner 81). Celan's relationship to *Hochdeutsch* is uniquely fraught. "Although exposed to and fluent in multiple languages (translating the works of no less than 43 poets in his lifetime), Celan adopted High German, the language in which his mother had culturally raised and loved her only child, as his 'mother tongue'" (Nieuwenhuis). This language and culture was part of the identity of the Jewish bourgeoisie in his hometown of Czernowitz. Yet, *Muttersprache* carries a depth of trauma when it also becomes *Mördersprache* (Buck). "Paul Celans Muttersprache war Deutsch. Und er schrieb in der Sprache der Mörder seiner Mutter" ("Paul

Celan's mother tongue was German. And he wrote in the language of his mother's murderers") (Böttiger). For Celan, however, engagement with the German language was a necessity, as he shared with a person close to him: "[o]nly in the mother tongue can one speak one's own truth, in a foreign language the poet lies" (Joris 16). In Celan's project, the German language must be confronted by dissecting it. Through that process, Celan could begin to construct a language for what could not be said.

George Steiner, in discussing Celan's often torturous relationship to the German language, has suggested that "every Celan poem is translated into German, and that in this process the receptor-language becomes unhoused and fractured … Nowhere is this theory of a Celanesque meta-German more applicable than in the poet's final volumes" (Steiner). Charlie Louth argues that Celan's 1971 work, *Schneepart* (*Snow-Part*), is written in "a language that is already in itself troubled and inflected by other tongues, and, spinning out a characteristic of language in general, [that is] intrinsically involved in acts of translation" (Louth). That is, as Celan, a translator of multiple languages, is writing he is already translating his thoughts into an idiosyncratic German. His later work also contains traces of multiple other languages, and "Celan's usage isn't confined by current norms" of his time. Furthermore, just looking at the title, Louth argues that *Schneepart*,

> . . . reaches down through the strata of words (where *Part* in German certainly has the main French sense of a share or portion), and, even more importantly in this case, obliquely out towards the neighbouring deposits of other languages. *Schneepart* is quite possibly intended, and can in any case be read, as the running together of French and German (and English) into one word. (Louth)

As a writer/translator reaching toward "the strata of words," Celan translates silence into his own idiom through both combining and fragmenting languages.

Sometimes, then, expression can be enhanced through "breaking" language. Nicholas J. Meyerhofer maintains that in Celan's later work, "His poetic idiom is here characterized by syllablized words, hermetic combinations and neologisms, all expressed in a (frequently) broken syntax" (Meyerhofer 9) that Steiner calls "idiosyncratic almost to the point of noncommunication" (Steiner 389). German words are broken as if to sever their relationship from the history they created, specifically the Holocaust. "Through language he attempted to remember [the Holocaust] and, at the same time, to remove it from all memory, so that the world could continue" (Exner 79). By shattering this language of death, Celan can paradoxically recoup and reembody the lost Holocaust victims. For example, in "Keine Sandkunst Mehr" ("No More Sand Art") Celan gradually diminishes the word "Tiefimschee" ("deep snow" or "deep in snow") to "Iefimnee" then "I—i—e." Franke calls this process "dismembering, maiming, and wounding words" (146), which can also extract new meanings.

Quite similarly, Michael T. Carter asserts that the voice in *The End of the Alphabet* is "[a]nguishing and fragmented," as "the voice in these poems relies heavily on broken syntax, unreliable grammatical structures—open parentheses and hyphens abound—because inner and outer forms have collapsed" (Carter 222). Yet, to wound or cut words—or the body—opens them up, creating space and allowing a view inside. Rankine also wounds or opens language through the use of ellipses, dashes, blank spaces, and blank lines. For example, the unspoken is indicated by an ellipsis: "Viewed in this way, / … her voice" (Rankine, *The End of the Alphabet* 9). Or, a long dash shows something cut off: "Dismiss the air and after her gesture, there, / the thrown off---" (9), the interruption made even more significant as the final line occurs at the bottom of the page. Or, an actual blank line shows something missing, or an answer that the reader may provide: "Where is the sea? / _____I will dance to the rhythm. You will play" (73). This quote also demonstrates the manner in which the poem creates connection: "I" dances to the "rhythm" that you "plays." Moreover, Rankine's title, *The End of the Alphabet*, suggests that the poet has gone to a place beyond conventional language: A place after the alphabet itself, the "end," indicating that having used every letter (and their possible combinations) the poet still cannot render into conventional speech that which remains unsayable. Rankine runs through the entire alphabet to recoup the knowledge in the female body, but having reached the "end," she then goes beyond closure to create a new form of communicability.

Totaling 100 pages, *The End of the Alphabet* is divided into twelve sections, what some may call lyric sequences. The shortest of these sections comprises four pages; the longest, ten. The first section, "Overview is a place," is four pages, as is the final section, "The quotidian." The section titles offer insights into the book's form and themes. For example, considering a book's front matter in the traditional sense, the reader might expect an "overview" that opens a book to contain an introduction or summary. Here, however, the opening section indicates that "Overview is a place." Significantly, the place suggested is the physical body, for in this poem, the body is the place from which language emanates. The mind fails us in the attempt to communicate that which is forbidden, secret, or outside of traditional mores that structure what can be said.

Or, in the "quotidian," section twelve, emphasis is drawn to the fact that the poem will consider the seemingly ordinary or mundane. This concern is emphasized in her most recent writing which demands that everyday encounters be examined to redetermine power relations. The longest sections are the fourth,

"Toward biography," and the seventh, "Residual in the hour." Ten pages each, they are placed near the book's center. The "residual" in section seven emphasizes that the poem will consider the left over, surplus, or excess. Finally, "toward biography" is an important clue to the poem's form and genre: while there are gestures "toward" the biographical, the poem is not centered on a unified subject, sometimes assumed to be a product of lyric expression, such as that which can be located in some of her earlier work, or in confessional poetry.

This chapter considers the book as one long poem, with twelve sections. In contrast, literary scholar Seanna Sumalee Oakley calls the sections "chapters," as in the continuous, interlinked portions of a novel, contending that *The End of the Alphabet* consists "of untitled poems divided into titled chapters or sections" (111), while poet and critic Calvin Bedient asserts that the "twelve titled sections [are] made up of separated but untitled sub-poems" (Bedient). While appearing "separate" on the page, the sections accrue meaning through the continuous reading of all twelve, making the poem book-length, not a collection of individual poems to be extracted.

In *Forms of Expansion: Recent Long Poems by Women* (1997), Lynn Keller argues that the long poem has an expansive "formal and structural range," including formalist writing such as the sonnet sequence, originated in the fourteenth century; the Classical epic that was remade into the "collage long poem" of the modernist epic; or the form of the lyric sequence, amongst others. (Keller 155). Keller, Susan Stanford Friedman, and other scholars also call into question "the prestige, the scale of achievement associated with the genre" of the long, big, or epic poem in part by removing assumed linkages between these kinds of poems and both whiteness and maleness (Keller 4–5). Rankine carries forward the lineage of the female epic from the eight distinctive women poets Keller analyses,[3] who expanded the long poem tradition in the 1980s and 90s.

In section one of the long poem, "Overview is a place," the work of silence and estrangement from the self is already underway. Indeed, for Rankine, the struggle to come to utterance begins with the book's first line: "Difficult to pinpoint," which is followed by white space and then another short line, "fear of self, uncoiled" (Rankine, *The End of the Alphabet* 3). This raises the immediate question: what is difficult to pinpoint? We begin our reading in an uncertain location; there is no place to land. Moreover, the book's opening does not conjure a singular voice; rather, it encourages us to consider what might make it impossible to inhabit the speaking subject at all. If we read across the enjambment of the opening lines we might also consider how it is difficult to pinpoint "fear of self." Rankine's poem opens engagement with subjectivity by questioning the existence of a stable sense of selfhood, where fear and trauma collide with representations of an assumed unified self. In literary trauma theory, as Michelle Balaev explains, "The idea that traumatic experience pathologically divides identity is employed by the literary scholar as a metaphor to describe the degree of damage done to the individual's coherent sense of self and the change of consciousness caused by the experience" (Balaev 150). Rankine's work in *The End of the Alphabet* demonstrates how to write from within that changed consciousness.

This is demonstrated through her choices of verbs; for example, the fear of the self is "uncoiled" in the poem. The speaker does not rest at the barrier that silence creates (the fear), but instead attempts to open up space for language, a process

---

3. Keller's study includes long poems by Sharon Doubiago, Judy Grahn, Rita Dove, Brenda Marie Osbey, Marilyn Hacker, Susan Howe, Dahlen, and Rachel DuPlessis. Other innovators of the long poem tradition include Theresa Hak Kyung Cha and Myung Mi Kim.

described in the vocabulary of the poem in a variety of ways as "uncoiling," "unstringing," and "unspooling." What might be seen as an intricate process of uncoiling springs or pulling threads is violently disrupted at the end of page three, however, with the following line: "bullet templed. rip the mind out. go ahead" (3). The attempt to unwind the threads of the self ultimately results in a physical gesture of ripping the mind out of the body, initiated with the violence of a weapon. It is in the body itself, not the mind, that the poet attempts to find language, for, as the speaker notes in "*Cast away moan,*" section four: "as much as I love the mind / it is there we lose" (84). Consciousness and the ability to speak are drawn in this poem from the body, rather than the mind, which is the place where "we lose" the ability to speak, "suggesting *once upon a time,* our addiction to telling, / is all effort to shape what surfaces within the sane" (23). "Addiction" to narrative, however, is an effort to shape experience into what is considered "sane" by the societal mind and thus fails to accurately represent individual experiences of trauma. Instead, Rankine seeks to "intersect into another's consciousness" with "the flux of feeling, and thought" (Rankine, "Claudia Rankine" 150). "This movement," Rankine contends, "has the particularity of fingerprints" (Rankine, "Claudia Rankine" 150). The language of consciousness is worn on the body.

Celan breaks apart the German language to render the unspeakable visible in an idiosyncratic language difficult even for German speakers to reconstruct into a recognizable form, and Rankine rips apart the body, tearing out the mind to reconstruct a language residing in "her insides." The process of generating language "from her insides" is necessarily violent. In "Overview is a place," for example, we witness "vertebral breaking," as the speaker attempts to crack open the body to find language (5). Additional physical violence is described as tongues are snipped out. Moreover, the throat itself is damaged by thought, indicating the need to move out of the mind and into the physical body (4).

...The moment

of elucidation snipped its tongue, its mouth water
dried out—
thought-damaged throat. (4)

The attempt to elucidate or explain actually injures those parts of the body—tongue, mouth, throat—needed to produce language. What is needed instead is the release of the mind's primacy over the body: "Lower the lids and the mind swims out into / what is not madness, and still the body / feels small" (19). The body feels small, yet it is where sense can be located. It is the place where the speaker must go to find something other than madness, for both the mind and language are wounded.

Of *The End of the Alphabet*'s protagonist, Rankine states, "I was experimenting with the idea that emotion could generate language. I wanted to create a 'languaged self' that was built up from her insides, from her pulse and breath" (Rankine, "Claudia Rankine" 148). This conjures Celan's "Atemwende," the turn of breath that pulses around words that transforms meaning. Locating language within the body in *The End of the Alphabet*, the speaker relates, "I coach myself, speak to my open mouth," (10) which renders speech separate from a mouth that opens to speak (she speaks *to* her mouth). The speaker must "coach" herself "from her insides" as "this life offering sorrow as voice" (12) is located in the feelings within the body, not a mind that generates words. Language, rather, emanates from the wounds stored in the body.

This wounding, according to Balaev's definition of trauma, "refers to a person's emotional response to an overwhelming event that disrupts previous ideas of an individual's sense of self and the standards by which one evaluates society" (Balaev 150). In *The End of the Alphabet*, the social conventions of womanhood are confronted by presenting a female body that is non-reproductive, outside the conventional role of motherhood, which bestows the female body with societal meaning and value, according to traditional gender roles. Not fulfilling the expectation of that role results in retribution. For example, there are indications in the text that the woman, or her body, is to blame for not giving birth to a child, such as when the doctor in the ninth section, titled, "Extent and root of," asserts, "...we can get in the way / of the umbilical cord and waste what is" (46). Getting "in the way" can be read as creating an obstruction that causes her to "waste" the pregnancy. Telling someone that they are "getting in the way" is usually an accusation, followed by a demand that they get "out of the way." Has she taken actions that result in getting in the way, or is her body itself being accused?

In *The End of the Alphabet*'s tenth section, "Residual in the hour," the male partner of the central speaker/protagonist ponders the loss of the child.

Later in a bar with a friend. He muses: There we were,
two children really.

Later in a bar with only one question. It begins: If we had had
the child—It ends: could he have shielded her from herself? (60)

Yet, the potential trauma of having the child is also considered, as he wonders if he could have protected her—even from herself. Moreover, the woman in the text is potentially faulted, or even disgraced, for seemingly choosing herself above others, which is not what a mother is expected to do.

Similar is the journey from not imagined to conceivable:
touch sinks, and innocence rolls over
residue, falling. Then to want; and in feeding the self

also to feed another, but at any moment to have chosen the self only: without emphasis, staring at nothing, though deepest is the taste in my mouth: sour. Despite the presence of others, spit. (47)

Despite the possibility of conceiving (becoming pregnant) and the expectation of tending to others, she has chosen herself, recovering agency even as she vomits into a sink. Or, moving from not being able to imagine the idea of motherhood, to being able to conceive of it causes touch to "sink" when the speaker wants to hold onto something solid, as innocence "rolls over" and is lost.

In this same section, the subject considers the possibility of having been disgraced, while also refusing that designation.

(She would not see it if she had been disgraced she would not
see she would not put it in front she
would not have it put in front she said do not bring it to me
if she has been disgraced
she said remind me of something else
an actress or a place something (48)

The intrusive memory of the trauma replays itself in her mind and she wishes to be reminded of anything other than this trauma and fear within her. "Do not bring it to me" suggests the left over, or residual, physical remnants of a lost or aborted pregnancy, but also indicates a refusal to carry the "disgrace" of not carrying the pregnancy. The pregnancy is not "complete," which may make her an incomplete woman, a failure in body and in her expected societal role. Yet she refuses such judgements: "Do not bring it to me."

These wounds are visible as the self collapses. There are many indications that the subject positioning in the poem is being altered and undone, as the speaker considers what constitutes "she":

55

> A she collapsing. some possible. some coherence unfastened.
> nothing acceptable. nothing stitched together: (30)

If coherence is "unfastened" the speaker can find "some possible," that is, opening up what is usually forced into connection creates new possibilities, new uses for language. When "she" collapses, when the poet opens up grammar and syntax, instead of sticking to expected formal conventions, or when she does not "stitch" together a narrative façade, a new kind of sense can be made that more closely approximates subjectivity and experience than conventional lyric or narrative forms.

In moving away from narrative closure, Rankine's aim, as she describes it, was to "distress the reading experience" (Rankine, "Claudia Rankine" 150). In this process, words are "no longer markings to be skimmed over toward the close of an expected narrative... The reading experience then would be a journey into a process outside of the narrative plot-driven arc" (Rankine, "Claudia Rankine" 150-151). However, Rankine is not just dispensing with the "self"; she is taking a further step as she investigates how to render subjectivity even more intimately than in autobiographical, confessional poetry. "My desire [in *The End of the Alphabet*]," Rankine relates, "was to revise what it meant to be 'confessional' or autobiographical" (Rankine, "Claudia Rankine" 148). Rankine isn't eschewing the "self" but instead creating a new poetics of selfhood.

Thus, Rankine writes in section five ("Where is the sea?"): "*You* is the door / too difficult to enter" (74). One of the valences of "you" is the lyrical construction of the self (74). Yet, subjectivity cannot be entered simply by opening a "door" into experience.

What craziness, she? *Among others?*   —these
that have no mouth, speak out

whispering my name.   *You* is the door
too difficult to enter, so overly the struggle. Whoever happens

is no subject for this throat. No one knows—   *Come out*
of the rain— (74)

Enacting the absurd, the lines "-these / that have no mouth, speak
out / whispering my name" inverts the impossibility of speaking
without a mouth: a metaphor for the dilemma of writing silence.
Yet, Rankine creates a poetics of subjectivity in which speaking
without a mouth, or writing silence, *is* possible. What cannot be
uttered must nonetheless be expressed, even if the expected tools
(mouth, words) are rendered useless. Celan's metaphor for this
experience is "interdicted lips," literally, lips with no mouth.

Although "these" ("she? *Among others?*") whisper her
name, the name has no referent because the subject cannot be
located behind the door. In fact, the door cannot even be entered.
"*You* is the door / too difficult to enter." Also note in the passage
from the poem above that "Whoever happens" (not "whatever")
"is no subject for this throat," indicating a wounded, unstable
subjectivity. The multiplicity of "shes" (she, others, these, you,
whoever) mentioned in this one section cannot simply be spoken
of in the conventional language of experience, of what
"happens," for this would create a false coherence estranged from
reality and from the pulse and insides from which Rankine seeks
to write.

To account for this multiplicity, this "whoever," Oakley
suggests that this "book-length 'toward biographical' poem, as
[Rankine] puts it, . . . imagines not an allegorical protagonist, nor
a lyric I, nor a narrative autobiographical heroine but the
posture—or imposture—of a common horizon of commitments

for incalculably differential individuals" (Oakley 111-112). Rather than "incalculably different individuals," this chapter argues that Rankine is presenting a prismatic view of a fragmented individual, through offering multiple views of what or who might construct "she" or "I"; however, Rankine does so without presenting a predetermined self that can be represented in the narrative language of experience. This is a move away from the formula of "I experience X, therefore I am X" and a move toward inhabiting the unnamable. Experiences of trauma can fracture the self into multiple selves that cannot be unified. The speaker, called "Jane," asks herself: "What Jane must substitute for this year's substitute / for a mind intact? ..." (4). A new "Jane" is conjured each year to "substitute" for a mind that is not intact or undamaged. Each "Jane" is a false narrative to convey so-called sanity.

The theme of silence and trauma—what cannot be said— is carried forward in the poem with an examination of "sanity," through the concepts of aphasia and "hysteria." Poet and scholar Wayne Koestenbaum asserts that *The End of the Alphabet* participates "in the time-honored feminist tradition of appropriating the discourse of hysteria, a classic symptom of which, according to Freud and Breuer, is aphasia. Poets and critics, including H.D., Myung Mi Kim, Helene Cixous, and Anne Carson, have used aphasia—the inability to speak—as an expressive device." (Koestenbaum). Moreover, in the long history of the diagnosis of "hysteria," from Sigmund Freud, to its use today, the term has been used to blame and silence those given this label.

For example, as Freud linked hysteria with a history of sexual abuse, he "believed that actual abuses had occurred in these patients (the 'seduction' theory), but then blamed them for having deceived him on that issue, so that he subsequently launched a 'fantasy' theory to explain the development of hysterical symptoms..." (Bogousslavsky and Dieguez 109).

Scholar Elke Krasny notes that in the twenty-first century, the term is still used to cast aspersions on others, "Calling someone hysterical is a pejorative calling. Such callings are accusatory, insulting, spiteful, and hostile. Pejorative callings are a strategy employed to discredit others" (Krasny 127). Krasny argues that the term is used to attack "all those who call out the systemic violence of xenophobic, misogynist, racist neoliberal authoritarianism, right-wing populism and far right extremism" and thus is used as a weapon to silence those who express certain progressive viewpoints.

Silence, trauma, hysteria, and aphasia are interlinked in a central section in *The End of the Alphabet* representing the loss of a pregnancy. Oakley argues that images of both miscarriage and stillbirth occur throughout *The End of the Alphabet* (131). In addition, of the so-called "plot" of *The End of the Alphabet*, Bedient writes, "no one will find it quickly or easily. (Turn first to page fifty if you want some basic facts)." Page fifty is indeed significant, the heart of the hundred-page poem:

… The complete effect: criminally
subterranean: first towel. then plastic bag. blood
and the umbilical cord fragmented. Remaindered: Asphyxiation
elsewhere.) It isn't my death but I am deep in with it (50)

In fact, it is possible to argue that the poem centers on this representation of miscarriage, or perhaps abortion or stillbirth. As the umbilical cord is "fragmented," so, too, is the self. This section highlights the "remaindered," the left over, detritus, or garbage of fragments that are placed for disposal in a plastic bag. It is this central trauma that wounds language as the speaker—though alive—dwells deep within death, a state that is also "criminally subterranean" and must be hidden.

Images of death are frequent in the poem. For example, prior to this scene, carnage is forecast through a piling of images of vultures, dead bodies, and despair: "...the vultures wing-wrapped / in the trees and some form of despair, a body / lying dead, wind held, odor pulling out" (49). This central image of pregnancy loss, then, is bracketed with references to rot.

> ... April 22nd
> Xed out. Nine months to outstare
>   as each garbage truck
> coughs in its wide turn. Without hurry, they begin
> loading, like flood victims passing sandbags;
> already weary, they work in slow motion. ... (49)

The feeling of suffocation is strong, with references to coughing, flooding, and asphyxiating. As the speaker watches the garbage truck turn while drinking from a milk carton, the reader is also confronted with the sour stench of death: "odor pulling out" of the body that is "remaindered" or left over, parts discarded (49, 50). The reference to flood victims adds to the feeling of suffocation; they cannot pile the sandbags fast enough to stem the flow. The speaker confronts "... Reined in half-sewage / sickening, stiffening the jaw" as "A form of despair is / running over the mountaintop on the outskirts of the minute," illustrating the embodied experience of affective states, as the speaker must "outstare" the nine months that will not bring a baby. The due date is crossed out on the calendar. She confronts this knowledge with a stiffening jaw that cannot open to speak. (50).

The speaker also refers to a private "hysteria" that is "swollen" and "leaking," linking the themes of flooding, drowning, and emotional excess with the female body. Krasny contends, "Such a diagnosis of being over-emotional, of being out of control and unstable, is very much linked to the feminization the term "hysterical" engenders. Those who are hysterical can by no means be taken seriously" (Krasny 126). Rankine's speaker states,

Privately,

             dukes up, duel, or duck, beat on,
or laughter; swollen, leaking in
to appeal, *To die.*

For in the hysteria, craven.
To the life loved: I have given
my hand, my word:

solemn, the oath.   And yet, still here, I am (26)

These passages also add to the conflation of the womb itself with excess emotion and death. "[L]aughter, swollen, leaking" are all excess; they cannot be contained "leaking in / to appeal, *To die.*" However, while the hysteria is "craven," it is rewritten here from an appeal to death, to an oath to live, sworn on "my hand, my word." Despite the appeal the death, "still here, I am."

Bedient describes feeling in *The End of the Alphabet* as traveling between the womb and the mouth: "brightenings of the rough particles of glum feeling spread around anyhow, in the womb, in the mouth. … For this sorrow is both enormous and (so it must feel, however against hope) eternal." Bedient's comments foster meditation on the concept of the "wandering womb," which can be traced back to Ancient Greece and was later used as an explanation by Hippocratic writers who sought to fortify the belief that a woman's emotive process is an illness. For those writers, "since the womb is believed capable of movement around much of the body, these texts attribute a wide range of symptoms to womb movement" (King 14). Emotional disturbance is thus linked to the womb.

Female experience of so-called hysteria, excess emotion, and the poetics of silence provide a particularly strong link between *The End of the Alphabet* and poems by Gwendolyn

Brooks from her mid-century modernist work. In its examination and rewriting of "hysteria," Gwendolyn Brooks's *Annie Allen* (1949) is a precursor to *The End of the Alphabet*. As Julia Bloch shows, "Brooks originally intended to title this section ["The Anniad"] 'The Hesteriad,' after the central figure she originally named Hester Allen" (455). Titling the section 'The Hesteriad' would have allowed a number of direct effects, including, "reappropriating the cultural narrative of hysteria as a circumscribed feminine malady and redeploying it instead as a heroic narrative" (Bloch 455). In addition, "the original title would, like 'The Anniad,' have punned on Homer's *Iliad* or Virgil's *Aeneid* but also would have invoked the longer discursive history of hysteria, the female body, and emotional excess" (Bloch 455). Rankine's engagement with the language of hunger, desire, and emotional excess, or in a line from the poem, "emotion in a relationship with too much of itself," is so intensified that it also produces aphagia, the inability to swallow, in its subject.

Rankine writes:

In another language hunger might bring her to her feet
but there is no hunger in English. Desire, longing—
every emotion in a relationship with too much of itself.
Not unlike the aphid sucking sap, soon we are unable

to swallow: aphagia.

and its meaning: If she stabs her throat thirty times
(a stab at each year) she knows what would pour out
but what pours in?
What put her here brought her to the ground so to speak. (61)

The speaker cannot be nourished "not unlike the aphid suck sap." Nor can she swallow her own hunger, desire, and longing. Each feeling remains stuck in the throat, and thus, unable to be swallowed, can only be accessed by stabbing the throat. The meaning of each year of her life would then "pour out." The poem rests on the hinge between swallowing and not swallowing, between silence and speaking. In order to unstick what is caught in the throat, it is necessary to write in a wounded language.

In a similar response to trauma, in "Appendix to the Anniad," subtitled "leaves from a loose-leaf war diary," Brooks responds to "thousands—killed in action" in World War II, addressing the "untranslatable" that creates the "need to loiter a little among the vague."

> You need the untranslatable ice to watch.
> You need to loiter a little among the vague
> Hushes, the clever evasions of the vagueness
> Above the healthy energy of decay
> You need the untranslatable ice to watch
> The purple and black to smell.
> (Brooks, *Blacks* 110)

"Untranslatable ice" refers to the coldness of death and the distance a reader of the news of war feels from the unnamed "thousands." Additionally, D. H. Melhem reads the figure of the untranslatable ice as "the repression necessary to bear what cannot be shared," or what has been rendered unspeakable through large-scale trauma (69). Yet, the poem tells the reader that they *need* the untranslatable ice "to watch." Lacking a nameable grief, the reader must watch, using sensory experience, rather than speech, to approach incomprehensible loss. Likewise, the poem tells the reader, you need "the purple and the black to smell," stressing the knowledge of embodied, sensory experience that language has yet to translate. When language cannot conjure a stable language for trauma, Brooks issues a call to "loiter a little among the vague," in the absence of direct reference. Like Rankine, then, Brooks finds knowledge within the body to inhabit experiences of silence, making a poem that connects the dead with a voice, and the poem with its readers in a shared experience of grief.

Brooks also engages silence and silencing in other poems of the same period as *Annie Allen*. In a discussion of how Brooks uses the rhetorical device of apostrophe to address and anthropomorphize dead children in her poem, "The Mother," published in 1945 in *A Street in Bronzeville*, Barbara Johnson notes that "Brooks is presenting the self as eternally addressed and possessed by the lost, anthropomorphized other. Yet the self that is possessed here is itself already a 'you,' not an 'I'" (189). The poem begins starkly: "Abortions will not let you forget. / You remember the children you got that you did not get." The end rhyme, along with the internal slant rhyme of "got" and "get" stresses the eternal presence of the memory of "my dim killed children." Thereafter, in stanza one, four of the ten lines begin with an address to "you": "You remember," "You will never neglect," "You will never wind up," "You will never leave them" (Brooks, "The Mother"). The mother is addressed as a devouring figure, "Return for a snack of them, with gobbling mother-eye," that is distanced from the "I" that begins to speak in the second stanza (Brooks, "The Mother").

Both Brooks and Rankine diffuse the lyric "I" by presenting a subject that is already othered from the self, that is, an estranged "I." This is necessary in the poems to approach the experiences of pregnancy loss. As Rankine writes in section five, "Where is the sea?":

no one knows
but *you* is pulled together, alternatively . . . I and you and
she juxtaposed (75)

The self is "pulled together" from fragments that might create coherence, yet the alternative Rankine presents in the poem is that "I and you and / she" are "juxtaposed" instead of being collapsed into one.

As Brooks's poem, "The Mother" ends, Johnson concludes, that "vocabulary shrinks away" and finally, "the speaker has written herself into silence" (192). The "I" in the second stanza addresses herself, as she wrestles with how to articulate her experience, "what shall I say, how is the truth to be said?" This is another striking similarity to *The End of the Alphabet*. Each confronting different historical and personal traumas in their work, Celan, Brooks, and Rankine write into and through silence.

Yet inside a subjectivity labeled as "crazy," the estranged "I" in Rankine's poem assembles a form of survival.

the appeal:

The day I am at peace I will have achieved
a kind of peace even I know suggests I am crazy.
But, as it will be how I survive, I will not feel so. (51)

Here again, seemingly opposite concepts are engaged. The speaker can achieve peace, but this is a kind of harmony that only confirms her to be "crazy." Yet to be "crazy," in this situation is also to survive. This can be achieved only through "an intimate connection with what is stored in the body," reanimating the body torn apart through trauma (94) and rejecting the societal expectations of what it means for a woman to present herself as "sane."

At moments in the poem, the speaker is simultaneously inside and outside of her body, directing the distanced self to speak into her own ear: "… open your mouth / close to your ear: fear / in sanity lives" (5). These lines present three possibilities: fear lives in sanity, to be sane is to experience fear, or, she fears that insanity lives. Yet, fear and sanity must exist together. To deny fear is to deny the sanity of what the traumatized body knows. In an intimate connection with what is stored in the body, "you" can finally rescue herself as the poem concludes:

> So you, in the role as your own rescuer, trebled
> voice
> trying on happiness, groomed echo of another,
> look out for yourself, go outside. stand up. straighter. flirt. (94)

Retaining what is cast off, "the waste remembered—   through the body," a new form of selfhood emerges where it is possible to "look out for yourself" in a voice that is "trebled" or tripled, increasing its strength (82). This enables the possibility of going outside and engaging with others to "try on" happiness. This is the moment of encounter that the poem creates.

3

Contamination and "Poisoned Regrets": Mothers and Artists in Claudia Rankine's *PLOT*

> outside of this insular traffic a woman in pink
> underlining the alias gender. who is she really? call
> her. could you. Would you. call her. Mommy?
>
> (Rankine, PLOT 5)

While her previous book, *The End of the Alphabet* (1996), eschews narrative arcs and plots, her third book, *PLOT* (2001), takes narrative head on, considering the ways in which plots are structured, the insistence on the repetition of the word itself, and its capitalization, becoming a kind of visual pun pointing toward the multiple meanings of plot. *PLOT* differs from her previous books in other significant ways: it is the first of her books to introduce visual elements onto the page, a feature that becomes much more prominent in *Don't Let Me Be Lonely* (2004) and *Citizen* (2014), her "American Lyric" sequence. 103 pages, with nine sections and an "Afterword," *PLOT* employs multiple genres, including lyric, drama, narrative fragment, and text boxes. This chapter examines how Rankine employs these elements in *PLOT* to construct new forms not governed by biology or gender norms—contesting forms of female identities enforced through narratives about pregnancy and motherhood—by also moving beyond traditional uses of the page. Thus, Rankine interpolates the body of the mother and the body of the text. While the fetus begins to form, transforming the pregnant woman's body in the poem, Rankine works across forms and genres, transforming poetic form itself.

Throughout the poem, Rankine draws out the meanings of "form" and "transform," creating a pairing that elicits multiple readings. Emphasizing embodied form, or what is sometimes called "writing the body," the speaker of *PLOT* asks, "Is the new always a form of truce? a bruising?" (31). The new form emerges in the attempt to create a truce between two identities that cannot be reconciled—mother and artist—and the violence of this attempt leaves a mark, a bruise. Merging subjectivities, and the emergence of birth, mark both the physical and textual body. This "truce" leaves a visible "trace": the seams are ragged and visible as irreconcilable identities and fragmented narratives are stitched from lyric, dialogue, and prose. The attempt reveals its own failure: the maternal body becomes a site not only of vestigial violence, but also rot: "then hard not to notice the depth of rot at the fleshy roots," contamination, and "poisoned regrets" that the poem's speaker, called Liv, must navigate in her efforts to survive (Rankine, *Plot* 5).

Embracing multiple means of "plot," Abram Foley argues that the title "evokes ... the construction of a narrative, the site of a grave, and, within the work's telling, the space of the womb in which a child develops" (Foley 232). As a burial plot, pregnancy represents rot, death in life. What must die in order for the child to live? How can Liv manage to live? In the "Afterword," the speaker also addresses "plot" in apostrophe, presenting further definitions: "Oh, action of narrative Oh secret plan To chart To chart A small / piece of land" (100). As this selection illustrates, plot is not only the action performed by narrative. A plot is simultaneously a secret, a chart, and a possession, all of which point toward pregnancy and the child in this work: charting the growth of the fetus in utero, keeping pregnancy a secret, or the pregnant woman keeping secrets from both herself and others about her real feelings and conflicts.

Finally, does the pregnancy, and then the infant, possess the mother's body, or is a child the mother's possession? In her foundational essay, "On Being the Object of Property," legal scholar Patricia J. Williams presents widely disparate examples—

68

that of her enslaved great-great-grandmother, Sophie, and Mary Beth Whitehead, mother of "Baby M"—in which the law renders women powerless in their relation to their own children (Williams). Sophie's daughter, Mary, was taken from her to be raised as a house servant, while Whitehead was "obligated" in the eyes of the law to relinquish her child to William Stern, the biological father for whom Whitehead served as a "surrogate," according to a contract that posited that she "will not form or attempt to form a parent-child relationship with any child or children" (Williams 14). "In both situations," Williams writes, "the real mother had no say, no power; her powerlessness was imposed by state law that made her and her child helpless in relation to the father" (14). The legal system that decrees these mothers powerless is further dehumanizing for Black mothers, not allowing agency in relation to their own children.

Williams contends: "I would characterize the treatment of blacks by whites in the whites' law as defining blacks as those who have no will" (9). As critical race theory shows, laws that may seem to be written as to apply to every person equally actually create systems of inequality, based here on both gender and race. Moreover, a form of feminist analysis called intersectionality also shows "that patriarchy interacts with other systems of power—namely, racism—to uniquely disadvantage some groups of women more than others" (Cooper 387). This is not a new concept; rather, it has roots in "a long history within black feminism's intellectual and political traditions," which, as Brittney Cooper demonstrates, goes as far back as 1892 to Anna Julia Cooper's work, *A Voice from the South by a Black Woman of the South* (Cooper 387).

Amongst Rankine's books, *PLOT* is distinctive because its larger formal structure (nine sections plus the Afterword) is in part predetermined by the subject—the nine months of pregnancy and the birth of a child—and the book is written in conversation with outside texts, including two works by Ingmar Bergman and

Virginia Woolf's novel, *To the Lighthouse*, from which Rankine borrows characters and themes. The allusions to Bergman and Woolf provide a textual foundation for *PLOT*'s examination of relationships and individual identities within the bourgeoise family, in particular the contradictions, split identities, and conflicts produced by the multiple affiliations and responsibilities that women artists face when they become mothers. In a new literary form sprung from following a new plot for pregnancy, Rankine employs dialogue, boxes of text or "word paintings," and textual fragments: plotting out the pregnancy while displaying the fragmentation of subjectivities that this plot elicits. The book is one long poem, presented in sections.

Rankine borrows characters and themes from her source texts to present the ambivalence, and real world challenges, that the artist who becomes a mother faces as she confronts these two, often incommensurate identities, as well as the inherent difficulties that pregnancy and motherhood create for producing art at all. To illustrate the complexities of the interrelationship between individual gender identity and social constructions of gender, gender is not assumed in *PLOT* and does not easily correspond to the societal expectations associated with binary gendered identities. Rather, gender is an "alias," a false or assumed identity (Rankine, *Plot* 5) that struggles to find expression through a language self.

PLOT remains understudied and is one of the least known of Rankine's books. Reviewers at its release lacked context for this work and several reviews were unfavorable. For example, reviewers at *Publishers Weekly* criticized *PLOT* for "run-on, obfuscated formulations and grammatical constructions" and struggled with how to connect the different generic elements, causing them to conclude that "it doesn't quite hit the mark" ("Poetry Book Review"). However, editors Erica Hunt and Dawn Lundy Martin included selections from *PLOT* in their 2018 collection *Letters to the Future: Black Women/Radical Writing*

(Hunt and Martin) instead of Rankine's recent, more lauded work, indicating a renewed interest in *PLOT* and its complexities.

From the first page—and with only two words and one punctuation mark—Rankine raises questions about genre and narrative.

PLOT

:

Inverse (Rankine 1)

"Inverse" according to the *Oxford English Dictionary* (*OED*) is something "[t]hat is or has been turned upside down; turned over" ("Inverse, Adj. and n."). Rankine's project does not simply reverse plot: it turns it over to see what is underneath, and what is inside, that the reader might not expect. A secondary definition of "inverse" includes "having the opposite or contrary nature or effect" ("Inverse, Adj. and n."). Using this definition, the book presents a form that is the opposite of "plot." The phrase "contrary nature," applies to matters of conventional literary forms—her innovative use of multiple genres that combine and invert recognizable forms—but also, within the poem, suggests that pregnancy itself is contrary to nature, inverting popular narratives of motherhood. Rankine's strategy of combining literary forms to achieve these effects is also evident on the first page, as critic Caitlin Newcomer and others note: the book is not only the inverse of plot, but also "a plot in verse," (363) reviving the productive tension between lyric and narrative that Rankine began working with in her first book, *Nothing in Nature is Private* (1994), and that is a prominent feature of *The End of the Alphabet*.

If we read Rankine's books in order, *PLOT* can be read as a sequel to the previous book, *The End of the Alphabet*, in its writing of the female body. While *The End of the Alphabet* dwells in the realm of the non-reproductive female body and the effects of pregnancy loss, *PLOT* obsessively writes the pregnant female body. In fact, the "Afterword" to *PLOT* seemingly refers to the pregnancy loss in *The End of the Alphabet* with a reference to "that other" who "gave up on the bright answer and passed so / Quickly beyond the umbilical, the walling flesh" (101) and also directly to "the stillborn one" (102).

> However . . . for all the Years lived attrition is still all, all needed
> though that other gave up on the bright answer and passed so
> Quickly beyond the umbilical, the walling flesh (101)

The definitions of "attrition" most helpful here include: "[b]reaking, fragmentation, or crushing of tissue; an instance of this," or simply, "[t]he action or process of wearing something down or away by friction; abrasion" ("Attrition, n."). Both of these definitions conjure rotting flesh and crushed identities. However, the breaking of tissue from the umbilical cord and uterine wall that appears in *The End of the Alphabet* as a stillborn child is, in *PLOT*, "saved": "Then she says, *The one that wasn't born, the stillborn one, was / saved.* One has to be born, I say" (102). Despite the nascent optimism in these lines, the plot of Liv's pregnancy is also filled with potential dangers that she must be warned against: "Liv is feeling in vitro. duped. a dumbness of chimes. no / smiles for every child so careful. so careful" (7). Liv is feeling "duped," made dumb, as she feels herself alienated from, or outside of, her own body, but she is also "assaulting the changing conditions," emphasizing the link between pregnancy and violence (7). However, she must be careful to offer "smiles for every child" as is expected from the mother figure.

The assertion that "one has to be born," is significant in the birthing of children, as well as creating art, particularly writing and painting, which are central to this "plot." On this theme, *PLOT* stresses the doubling of "generating" and "generations." The generating of art and literature is crucial to generating new ideas and identities, connecting to previous and future generations of women artists and writers, and creating familial generations by birthing children. "The drive in utero is fiction-filled. arbiter of the cut-out infant. and mainstreamed. Why birth the other. To watch the seam rip. To roughly conjoin the lacerating generations?" (Rankine, *Plot* 5). While it is easy to read the term in the first phrase as "friction filled," an intentional rhyme that dovetails with the viciousness of the phrases "cut-out," "seam rip," and "lacerating," the phrase is actually *fiction-filled* (emphasis added) showing the violence that can be inflicted by fictions of motherhood that are forced upon women. The "drive in utero," that generates violence—cuts, rips, and lacerations—is also a place that generates fictions, some of which are societally generated and must be confronted.

One reviewer speculates: "This book seems consciously aimed at the nexus of several different feminist avant-garde projects, from the nouveau roman of Monique Wittig to Theresa Hak Kyung Cha's *Dictee*" ("Poetry Book Review"). Cha's *Dictée* represents bodies not only through language, but also through family photographs and other visual media, including an acupuncture chart, and images made using photocopies, what Alison Fraser identifies as "xerography" (31). Like *Dictée*, Rankine's *PLOT* participates in a tradition of innovative long poems by women that contain multiple generic, as well as visual elements, pointing back to Muriel Rukeyser's social documentary poetry in the 1930s, a form that Rankine also embraces in *Don't Let Me Be Lonely* and *Citizen*.

If *PLOT* is understood within an American modern and contemporary long poem tradition—particularly that created by women—it is easier to discern how the book's seemingly separate parts work together as a whole. Just as Rukeyser's documentary poetry must be placed in its socio-historical context, so, too, as Alison Fraser argues, Cha's project must be placed within its context: the Japanese occupation of Korea and the ensuing Korean diaspora. "Within a context where Korean identity is continually suppressed, the minutiae of material life—family photographs, diary entries, letters, official government documents—gain significance where they might otherwise be overlooked" (31-32). In real-life experiences in which self-ownership of one's language (the Japanese forbade use of the Korean language) and one's body are not allowed, documentation can create "sites of self-possession" and invert power relations (32) a strategy inherent in *Don't Let Me Be Lonely's* documentation of personal ephemera.

In Section 2 of *PLOT* (indicating the second month of pregnancy) the plot's main character, Liv, considers the pain of the loss of individual identity that can occur with motherhood, the pregnant woman becoming a mere vessel for the child, instead of her own person.

> … mother coded
> for other, a gate only, a mighty fortress, a door swinging open …
>
> or is she that—that vessel, filling up, swelling to overflow until
> mothery is the drowned self, drowning all that is, all that clings? (18)

The mother is "coded" or programmed "for other." She exists only to serve others. Furthermore, she exists for reproduction, her body "a gate only" that opens to birth a child. She is also a symbol of excess, overflowing emotion resulting in motherhood which is "drowning all that is." In addition, the "drowned self," is a theme that recurs throughout the poem (and will be emphasized, beginning in Section 4 with references to Woolf's character in *To the Lighthouse*, the painter Lily Briscoe, as well to Woolf herself). There is not a way in this selection to reimagine forms of motherhood in which "mothery" is *not* the drowned self.

The drowned self, or what Newcomer calls "the 'I' [that] disappears," haunts Liv as she contemplates the possible destruction of the self by all-consuming motherhood (366). "Then it is as if the hood of motherhood was meant to blur herself from herself, a dark cloth dropping over her eyes until the self of selfless near arose" (Rankine, *Plot* 20). Narratives of motherhood can overwhelm and destroy "I" so that the self is estranged, "meant to blur herself from herself." Motherhood becomes a hood, "a dark cloth" so that the woman's self is impossible to see, even from within, as the "self" is replaced with selflessness. This is also rendered textually as the unborn's "plot." Bonnie Blader explains how the plot follows "Liv, recording her resistance and submission to the idea of her unborn son, Ersatz, who inhabits her, body and mind, and plots to be born" (Blader). Rather than suffering erasure with the birth of a child, Liv attempts to find a way to write (and paint) herself back into this plot, to be seen and preserved.

At the beginning of the book, the idea of a child is presented through a dream in which a baby is not a sentimental notion; on the contrary, the fetus is a kind of alien with "freakish anatomy" contaminating the woman's body, and filiation—or the relationship of child to parent—is artificial, "hard plastic." The alien form occupies the woman's body.

Submerged deeper than appetite

he bit into a freakish anatomy. the hard plastic of filiation.
a fetus dream. once severed. reattached. the baby femur
not fork-tender though flesh. the baby face now anchored. (4)

The dream about the fetus is fitful, "severed" then "reattached." The fetus is inhuman before assuming personhood when "the baby face" becomes "anchored." While the text insists that what the mother "would make would be called familial. not foreign," the effects of pregnancy on the woman's body are also referred to in Section 1 (the first month of pregnancy) as "the hormonal trash

75

heap howling back," poisoning the body as rotting "trash" (6). The poem brings into focus the often messy physical realities of the pregnant body, a body that can feel foreign to the pregnant woman experiencing its changes, with the biological realities of the "trash heap." The pregnancy becomes contamination, making some pregnant women very ill as if their bodies are occupied by an alien other. Liv's own body is giving way to the fetus's growing parts (femur) before she can imagine a child's face.

The layering of multiple texts in *PLOT* engages literary possibilities that Rankine creates through conversations with outside sources, intertextual leaps that echo further meanings. In addition to her reading of Woolf, Rankine explains that at the time of writing *PLOT*, she was watching all of Swedish director Ingmar Bergman's films (Rankine, "Poetry Daily Prose Feature: Interview with Claudia Rankine"). She notes the particular influence of *Scenes from a Marriage*, a TV mini-series released in 1973, which Bergman asserted was about "the absolute fact that the bourgeois ideal of security corrupts people's emotional lives, undermines them, frightens them" (The Ingmar Bergman Foundation, "Scenes from a Marriage") and the 1957 film, *Wild Strawberries*. *PLOT* embodies the corrupting and frightening influence of the bourgeois family, a narrative that plots to steal a woman's agency.

Considering which of her source texts most influenced the construction of her imagined plot of pregnancy and family making, Rankine maintains that: "... Bergman's film *Wild Strawberries* probably influenced the plot of *PLOT* most" (Rankine, "Poetry Daily Prose Feature: Interview with Claudia Rankine"). The film centers around two characters, Professor Isak Borg and his pregnant daughter-in-law, Marianne, who is unhappy and planning to separate from her husband, Evald (Isak's only son), but the main conflict in the film between father and son. The film's plot also contests relationships between fathers and mothers in the heterosexual nuclear family unit. *Wild*

Strawberries is also about "portraying oneself in two versions," which echoes the doublings present throughout *PLOT*, (The Ingmar Bergman Foundation, "Wild Strawberries") as Liv, the main character in Rankine's *PLOT*, ruminates on what it will mean to be both an artist and a mother. Doublings occur through the poem on the linguistic level as well: Liv/live form/transform, truce/trace, and others.

Meant to provide security, the isolated family unit can instead undermine emotional health. Thus, "Rankine's persona in *Plot* (2001) ... is apprehensive about the possibility of locating her poetic identity within the currents of mainstream cultural narratives. The poems as a whole show that the fragmented female experience is already a subjective experience within the subconscious recesses of the poetic mind" (Morrison 7). Moving fragmented female experience out of the subconscious into the languaged self transforms the way the plot can be told, replacing plots that are inadequate for creating space for a pregnant woman's individual subjectivity.

Bergman's work not only provides Rankine with an example of how to consider multiple versions of the self within one work of art, but also is also the source of the names of two of her principal characters: "The characters' names in *PLOT* came from the names of the actors in *Scenes from a Marriage*, Liv Ullmann and Erland Josephson. I loved that Erland sounded like 'her land' and that Liv dovetailed into *life, live, livelihood*." (Rankine, "Poetry Daily Prose Feature: Interview with Claudia Rankine"). Liv and Erland are thus the names of the mother and father in *PLOT*. Little attention has been given, however, to the significance of the name of the child in *PLOT*: Ersatz.

While "Ersatz" is lexically similar to "Erland," that of the father in *PLOT*, and also to "Evald," the name of the son in *Wild Strawberries*; crucially, the meaning of the word "Ersatz" is: "A substitute or imitation (usually, an inferior article instead of the real thing)" ("Ersatz, n."). Thus, if the child is a double for the art object, the son's name is strongly indicative that in a choice between art and motherhood, the substitution of the child for the woman's creative work is an inferior choice. The book struggles with the proposition of how to live a life in which Liv does not choose just one or the other, which would cause her individual subjectivity to die, but instead, somehow holding onto art and self with the birth of a child. The poems examines Liv's often painful conflicts as she struggles to do so.

Early sections of the poem also suggest that the child is an indiscretion, and somehow unnatural, untouched by "natural light." This narrative opposes those that present pregnancy, child bearing, and motherhood as "natural."

Ersatz

This. his name said. Afterward its expression wearing
the ornate of torment. untouched by discretion. natural light
or (so rumored (7)

Working with the lexical proximities of "ornate" and "torment"—"what Rankine has called the trace elements in words, how one word has a sound memory of other words in it, although their meanings may not be similar"—Rankine displays the contradictory emotions that saying the child's name aloud elicits in Liv (Blader). Rankine explains how the choice to use lexical similarities throughout the poem relates to the book's content: "The idea with *PLOT* was pregnancy, so the thought was quite literally: how many things engender an other? How can the subject inform the form? Since *PLOT* was an investigation of shape within shape, and language was my tool—the words became lives themselves, and I began to see words within words" (Rankine, "Poetry Daily Prose Feature: Interview with Claudia Rankine"). Thus, considering her pregnant body, Liv contemplates the literal experience of a body within a body, as well the subjective experience of the artist considering the costs of her own subjectivity being superseded by the subjectivity of her child-to-be as "torment" and "poison."

The metaphorical doubling of poem and child in women's poetry is older than the American nation itself as is evident in Anne Bradstreet's poem "The Author to Her Book" (1678) wherein she addresses her book as an "… ill-form'd offspring of my feeble brain, / Who after birth didst by my side remain" (Bradstreet). Bradstreet's rhetorical conceit is dependent on the mother/poet being ill-equipped properly to revise and present a beautiful poem/child, in the words of Bradstreet, the inability to "[t]hy blemishes amend." The speaker of Bradstreet's poem reports, "I washed thy face, but more defects I saw / And rubbing off a spot still made a flaw," and thus her book is but "My rambling brat (in print)" with an irksome visage and uneven "feet," a reference to the poem's meter (Bradstreet). Similarly, Ersatz is used in *PLOT* to represent both poem and child, with the nine sections of the poem acting as a textual double for the nine months of transformation of the pregnant body.

PLOT presents a number of other doublings and multiplicities, which are enabled in part by Rankine's use of shifting pronouns. "Much of the poem refers to Liv in the third person," argues Newcomer,

but this is often complicated by shifts into moments clearly voiced by Liv's "I" or moments wherein the speaker's relation to both this "I" and this "she" is ambiguous . . . creating a poetic voice that is paradoxically doubled, both self and 'other,' a doubled sameness that mirrors Liv's continual questioning of her relationship to Ersatz. (Newcomer 363)

The shifting of pronouns also allows the reader to witness Liv's changing feelings toward the transformations taking place in her body. In Section 1, the speaker, referring to Liv in the third

79

person, explains the conflicts she feels at the beginning of her pregnancy: "Once Liv thought pregnancy would purify. You Ersatz / effacing. her pace of guilt. her site of murmur" (7). While "efface" means to obliterate or to make oneself insignificant, it is also used in obstetrics to describe the process by which the uterine muscles and cervix are "distorted" in preparation for labor ("Efface, v."). Here, Rankine is considering how pregnancy may cause a woman's identity, as well as her physical body, to be both effaced and distorted, positing pregnancy as a site of spoilage and disfigurement, rather than a state that can "purify" womanhood.

The insertions of dialogue (usually conversations between Liv and Erland) externalize the internal dialogue continuing to run through Liv's mind, while at the same time giving a voice to Erland:

> What do you mean, are we sure?
> Just because we are pregnant doesn't mean we have to have it.
> What would we be waiting for?
> I don't know . . . to be sure? (13)

While Liv considers that they may need "[t]ime to understand how completely, completely changed our lives will be," Erland insists that while it will be scary, "...we will have our lives plus the baby," showing that Erland sees primarily what will be added to their lives by having a child, not what must be sacrificed (13). The poem shows, however, the real conflicts and choices that the woman artist confronts when making a family. Honing in more specifically on the writing of the pregnant body and the experience of mothering in her book of essays, *Translating the Unspeakable: Poetry and the Innovative Necessity*, poet Kathleen Fraser asserts that "the ambivalence for women artists around the issue of children and mates will never be resolved" (44). However, *PLOT* does reframe this ambivalence about pregnancy and motherhood, turning it also into generative possibilities.

These possibilities include new elements of form such as the overarching framing devices, as well as incremental moves on the level of individual words and punctuation. For example, the poem employs eye rhymes, puns, and full rhymes. "Proximity of Inner to In Her" uses the lexical proximities of "inner" (inner self) and "in her," a fetus literally inside her body, to show what is at stake: transformed subjectivity and a transformed body. Internal rhyme also provides emphasis: "how not to? When in utero a fetus heartbeat bounces off. / scanned vibrations of this newer soul making a self whole" (12). The "scanned vibrations" of an ultrasound provide evidence of a "newer soul" and the possibility of creating "a self whole." "A self whole" refers both to the fetus and the question of whether motherhood will diminish the "mothery" self, or lead to wholeness. Therefore, "a self whole" can also be read as "a self hole," or a hole where the self once was.

If one takes an "inverse" strategy to reading the book and considers the "Afterword" first, within that section are multiple definitions of "plot," as the child "plots" to be born. The pregnancy and the child now determine the parents' trajectory and how they will spend their days, causing them to lose time: "the child I am. structured the plot they lost time to" (100). The lost time may be the actual time preparing for, birthing, and caring for an infant, but it also points to a loss of the mother's singular identity: "*What is the world without I in it?* I who am nothing without plots / propping me up—" (100). The parents' world may be nothing without a child in it, and the mother is also considering what it means to lose "I," her own sense of self as she shifts from individual to mother. As is evident in this quote, adopting familial roles, in particular that of mother, may follow expected life narratives to prop up the characters and give them a sense of who they are. At the same time, one must also consider what may be lost when adopting conventional expectations of how one's life is supposed to proceed, being "propped up" as if utilizing props on the theatrical stage while playing a role.

Liv approaches the plot with contradictory emotions, including apathy, fear, and excitement.

> . . . This is it: a whole possible embodied by Liv and
> she now not caring, fearing, though nearing to meet it. In thought
> the thought is barely tolerated, ushered out, and still
>
> *oh, Liv,*
>
> must you insist on rot in the plot to continue? Must you turn life
> on its head, inverse the process, live its evil?" (25)

Will the "whole possible," the plot embodied by Liv in the physical form of her pregnancy, open up new options, or will it threaten Liv's existence? Yet, just considering her ambivalence, Liv is rebuked for "insisting" on the "rot in plot" and inverting "live" to "evil." It is as if she has sacrificed her own subjectivity—and her rights to question and feel—with her pregnancy. She is admonished for daring to ask the questions that she must consider about the changes that pregnancy and a child will bring. Yet the plot of pregnancy must move forward. Despite Liv's fears, and despite her existential questions, she is "nearing to meet it," that is, moving closer to the birth of her child. The physical body will win out in the execution of a linear plot. There must be some conclusion to the pregnancy, as the poem underscores, "we can't shake the natural course of things" in relation to how the fetus develops, unless of course, one chooses abortion (48).

PLOT employs boxes of text—along with allusions to the painting in *To the Lighthouse*, and the painting that Liv is creating throughout the poem—to explore the visual along with the textual. Variously sized boxes containing textual fragments first appear in Section 4 of *PLOT*. The few writings on *PLOT* are split concerning the effectiveness of this visual device. A reviewer for *Publisher's Weekly* argues: "A dialogical 'Interlude' and a series of odd, graphically charted pages chart further separations, but don't feel completely motivated" ("Poetry Book Review"). Newcomer reads what this reviewer calls "graphically charted pages" as a reflection of content, specifically the focus on painting: "These boxes are filled with floating words functioning as strokes of language" (Newcomer 367). In addition, Blader argues that *PLOT*'s "visual surprises, Rankine's use of block print, boxed text, full stops mid-phrase, open field, conversation, word paintings and proximities, all complicate 'Here' at the textual level" (Blader). The strategy of linking form with content through the use of "strokes of languages" or "word paintings" is a useful way of understanding how *PLOT* is informed by Woolf's *To the Lighthouse*.

Kate Jenckes argues that, "In the second trimester, rather than focusing directly on her pregnancy, Liv explores the nature of relation and survival through aesthetic inheritance, primarily through the figure of Virginia Woolf" (Jenckes 96). "Aesthetic inheritance" is another way to consider the making of generations. Liv's survival is strongly dependent on connecting to her female artistic ancestors who guide her in creating a new plot, using both painting and writing. The series of poems in Section 4 containing the word boxes is called "Eight Sketches / *After Lily Briscoe's Purple Triangle*" (370) and thus an explicit allusion to the unmarried painter in Woolf's 1927 novel, *To the Lighthouse*. Lily Briscoe struggles with her painting throughout the course of the novel as she battles societal attitudes toward women artists that she has internalized. In fact, a male character in the novel (Charles Tansley) specifically tells her, "women can't write, women can't paint" (292), and this phrase in repeated in various forms throughout the novel (Woolf). Lily Briscoe does nonetheless complete the painting by the novel's end, an important triumph in Woolf's fiction.

Painting mobilizes creativity in *PLOT*, moving Liv and the larger arc of the poem forward. Creativity rescues the plot from rot. Painting also drives the narrative force of *To the Lighthouse*. Scholar Cara Lewis argues that "the visual, particularly the still life," becomes "a visual force and a constituent part of the progress of the narrative" in *To the Lighthouse*, "from the dinner table to the children's nursery to the abandoned drawing room" all of which are interior, domestic spaces. Still life painting "also intermingles with the novel's range of affects, including sympathy, melancholy, and even more extreme states, like terror and inevitability of death." Thus, "the visual and affective concerns of the novel converge" (Lewis 426). The "word paintings" in *PLOT*, a new device for Rankine, and the very specific allusions to Woolf's novel, function in the same fashion, linking the visual with Liv's affective state.

In the form of the novel, Lewis explains, the standard analysis evokes the opposite, perceiving visual description as stasis: "Indeed, most foundational works of narratology have held that description and plot name forces working in opposite textual directions—that descriptions of all kinds constitute narrative stoppages... In short, from a classical narratological perspective, what happens in a description is nothing at all: happening and describing are incommensurate activities" (435). In contrast, Lewis contends that "in *To the Lighthouse*, verbalized visual forms exert great narrative force—what we might even think of as a kind of narrative determinism" (435). Thus, argues Lewis, "description and image may not merely parallel the plot of *To the Lighthouse*, but instead propel it" (435). This narrative force, Jenkins contends, "is evident only if we borrow an art historical mode of reading attentive to the traditions of still life painting. With this kind of reading we can see that, as literature mingles with the visual arts, it does not aspire to immobility or attempt to become primarily spatial instead of temporal" (Lewis 435), emphasizing the need for alternate reading strategies for literatures, including *PLOT*, that contain representations of visual art as a core elements.

Amber Jenkins also emphasizes movement and painting in *To the Lighthouse*, in her reading of the "embodied theory of aesthetics" she finds in the novel. "In her unification of politics and aesthetics in *To the Lighthouse*, Woolf poses a challenge to pure formalism's emphasis upon durable and static form by centralizing the palpability of both body and art in the physical connection between Lily and her painting" (Jenkins). In the ninth section of "The Window" this embodied movement is emphasized through the verbs "scraping," "force," "move," and "flow." "[S]craping her palette of all those mounds of blue and green which seemed to her like clods with no life in them now, yet she vowed, she would inspire them, force them to move, flow, do her bidding tomorrow" (Woolf 76). The movement is created by Lily's vow to "inspire" the mounds of paint. It is also at this point in the novel where Lily's "flow" is interrupted by William Bankes, illustrating the difficulty women artists confront in creating space for themselves within a patriarchal scheme. Or, as Jenkins explains: "Significantly, the moments at which Woolf highlights the physical connection between Lily and her painting are moments of male interruption." Liv confronts these moments of "interruption" likewise throughout *PLOT* as she surveys the elements of her creative process "with no life in them now." It is at these junctions that "rot" must be transformed into "plot," movement that allows Liv to transcend stasis.

Of Woolf's female characters, Theresa L. Crater argues, "[o]nly Lily Briscoe . . . [is] capable of articulating her vision of being a woman other than the prescribed role of Woman" and that "[b]y finishing her painting, Lily Briscoe expresses an alternative reality to the silencing role of Woman (Crater 121, 135). Some critics interpret the dark triangle (the purple triangle in Rankine's title) in Lily Briscoe's painting as a representation of Mrs. Ramsay, a character in the novel who represents a traditional feminine domesticity, in contrast to Lily's flaunting of gendered expectations. Mrs. Ramsay "serves her husband" by "constantly reassuring him that he is admirable, by giving him sympathy," but these and other relentless demands exhaust Mrs. Ramsay to the point that Lily observes that this incessant giving results in Mrs. Ramsay's death (Crater 126). But Lily also desires Mrs. Ramsay, creating an erotic connection between the two, further upending gender expectations. "Yet for all her acknowledgement of Mrs. Ramsay's faults, Lily is attracted to her physically ... and desires a more permanent union with her, one that will open the mind and heart of Mrs. Ramsay to Lily" (Proudfit 31). All of these themes are in play in "Eight Sketches / *After Lily Briscoe's Purple Triangle*." The plot of *To the Lighthouse* must come to a conclusion, as the making of the painting must also, linking Liv's struggle to paint to Lily's.

Rankine also considers representation of mothers and mothering through Woolf's Mrs. Ramsay and Lily Briscoe's painting: "A face as mother, a shadowing other, an unyielding / surface in waste and worse—purple" (41). Mothering here is depicted as unyielding and suffocating. Moreover, Rankine is alluding not only to the character of Lily, but also to Woolf herself, a writer who did not have children, but who succumbs to literal drowning at her own hand. Either side of the dilemma of whether to have children or not to have children can become suffocating for the female artist, thus thwarting the energy to live.

The text boxes reappear in *PLOT* in Section 6 as part of a series of poems entitled "Painting after the death of Virginia Woolf entitled / Beached Debris" (54). "She experiences and is herself as beached debris. of course. / of course" (54).

You, she says to the quiet reflecting Woolf's absorbed face, you are a log . . . a black log of soaked bark like floating fur.

And though Liv approaches willingly the gaping enigma
smoke-shading the muddy bank, its eroding shoreline, her
darkened heel, penciled in, relinquishes movement. (54)

Liv speaks to "Woolf's absorbed face" that she is creating on the
canvas, addressing the image as "you": "you are a log." Woolf's
drowned body becomes detritus floating in the water. The body is
alienated from the human, "a black log of soaked bark,"
described as "floating fur." Blader shows that "Liv paints and
repaints Virginia Woolf's drowned body floating, without
volition, in the River Ouse. *Plot*, she reminds us, rhymes with
rot" (Blader). For Liv, the "muddy bank" with its "eroding
shoreline" absent an image of Woolf as a live person becomes a
"gaping enigma," a gap where a person should be. The reference
to the floating log was introduced previously in Section 5 in the
form of a dialogue:

Here is a log . . . a black log of soaked bark like floating fur.

"What kind of log is that?"

"No log . . . a woman."

"A woman's body? Oh, right." (48)

When the "log" is recognized as human, it is an afterthought, "A
woman's body? Oh, right." One must be reminded that the body
was that of a woman. She easily disappears.

Liv faces a dilemma here, as the representation of a
mother's face and Woolf's drowned face both shadow her. The
mother and the artist: can she, Liv, be both? Can Liv remake
these concepts, and her own identity, through the process of
painting and repainting them? Can the mother and the artist both
survive? Inasmuch as *PLOT* is about birth, it is also about death.

Jenckes, writing about theorist Jacques Derrida's "Nightwatch" and Rankine's *PLOT,* names this positioning "a certain form of *life-death*" (Jenckes 93). "Contemplating her position between a dead writer [Virginia Woolf] and her unborn child," Jenckes writes, "Liv is able to consider how life, inheritance, and reproduction are not (only) rehearsals of plots, but also, inevitably, exposed to what comes—from both death and life, past and present, inside and out" (Jenckes 97). "*Life-death*" proposes that one experiences both states simultaneously.

Yet, what must die so that something or someone else may live? Liv survives to create this plot and through its focus on the creation of art, the poem demonstrates that acts of the creative imagination are necessary for the woman/artist/mother to find new ways of being, even as other deaths—of personality, agency, and life choices—must occur with the birth of a child. Writing and painting allow life to persist alongside death. "Art persists because it takes form and has an ending. Art, for Rankine, is deliberate and maintains a deliberative ethos that may be turned at once toward death and life, toward a memorial impulse that doubles as an affirmation of life" (Foley 233–34). This additional doubling, turning toward life and death simultaneously, shows that life may emerge out of death, as new identities are born.

These identities, and the ways they might fit together, are not simple; rather, women must actively participate in the process of creating and recreating them for themselves in each generation, drawing from the writers and artists before them, which the allusions to multiple texts demonstrate. In the twenty-first century United States, many women also find themselves having to fight for humane solutions to the weight of their multiple roles, due to American social institutions' refusals to provide basic supports for mothers and children (such as affordable, quality childcare or paid parental leave) or choices about their own medical care, leaving individual women with varied anxieties in isolation. Rankine's focus is smaller than this, more existential than practical. In some ways, the imagined woman/artist/mother Liv has a kind of luxury, the time and space of Woolf's "room of own's one," to ponder her existential dilemmas and changing identities. Yet Audre Lorde reminds us that "poetry is not a luxury." It is only through radical imaginative acts that a different future for the Black poet, the Black mother, can be conjured and put into action (Lorde, "Poetry Is Not A Luxury" 36-39).

Much like the concept of life-death, *PLOT* also offers present-future as simultaneous in its focus on generating and generations. Drawing on Friedrich Nietzsche concept of the "untimely," Foley argues that "Rankine's work shares Nietzsche's hopes to a degree: to act counter to the present for the benefit of a time to come," which "becomes not a deferral of life but an invitation to it" (234). Nietzsche writes that the untimely "acts counter to our time and thereby acts on our time and, let us hope, for the benefit of a time to come" (Nietzsche 60). Creating a generative female identity that can choose motherhood without drowning in the cultural expectations or economic imperatives of that role is indeed "counter to our time." The fight is continual, emerging, retreating, and emerging again. Feminist gains in expanding choices for women contract through anti-woman policy decisions. Thus, Rankine can draw no tidy conclusions; however, in Section 9 as the child is finally being born, Liv asks, "How will he feel to the touch?" and answers optimistically, "With him resides the best truth in the flesh" (97). Accepting the "invitation" that truth and hope may offer, Liv attempts to write a new plot that embraces "I," insisting on the choice to live.

Thus, though multiple conflicts are presented, *PLOT* also explores what generative possibilities might exist for the woman/artist/mother. Lorde states that poetry is "illumination" and uses the figure of the Black mother and the metaphor of birth to explain what must be done: "it is through poetry that we give name to those ideas which are, until the poem, nameless and formless—about to be birthed, but already felt. That distillation of experience from which true poetry springs births thought as dream births concept, as feeling births idea, as knowledge births (precedes) understanding" (Lorde, "Poetry Is Not a Luxury" 36). At the end of *PLOT* when the speaker declares, "One has to be born, I say" (102) "one" refers not only to the child, but also to the woman who must create, or give birth to, a new identity for herself. The poem works to make what was previously "nameless and formless" (Lorde, "Poetry Is Not a Luxury" 36) into knowledge and reality. The book's final line declares that one is "borne to a billion chances—" (Rankine, *Plot* 103). "Chances" here indicates not only accident and happenstance (those things we cannot choose about our lives), but also possible optimistic beginnings, opportunities to maintain agency and create something new.

4

Word, Image, Feeling: *Don't Let Me Be Lonely* and Social Documentary

Define loneliness?

Yes.

It's what we can't do for each other.

What do we mean to each other?

What does a life mean?

Why are we here if not for each other?

Don't Let Me Be Lonely (62)

Published in 2004 by Graywolf Press, Claudia Rankine's *Don't Let Me Be Lonely: An American Lyric* is the first of her books to contain a wide variety of multi-media images. Rankine began to expand her use of the page as visual field in *PLOT* (2001), with fragments of text framed in black boxes to create what might be described as "word paintings," but *Don't Let Me Be Lonely* is the first book to collage various found visual components into the text. These include a small, cube-like television; an x-ray; photographs; maps; prescription labels; and, a diagram of an artificial heart. Of these, the television is most ubiquitous, a realistic photographic image with black-and-white static on its screen, containing an undisclosed image of President George W. Bush that makes him part of the "white noise." Used to denote the book's section breaks, the television also displays scenes from movies and television news, as well as slogans from commercials. Like long, modernist poems and mid-century Afro-Modernist poems, such as Melvin Tolson's *Libretto for the Republic of Liberia* (1953), the book concludes with a substantial section of endnotes. Significantly, Rankine's themes in *Don't Let Me Be Lonely*, and her use of a variety of found documents and images continue the tradition of documentary poetry and other social documentary forms from the 1930s, updating the form to represent life in a multi-media era in which people have become heavily dependent on television viewing as both a leisure activity and source of information.

Don't Let Me Be Lonely examines illness—cancer, dementia, heart disease, HIV/AIDS—and dis-ease—loneliness, sadness, hopelessness—as both individual and social states of being and takes up, as an ethical question, the relationship between the self and others: "Why are we here if not for each other?" (Rankine, *Don't Let Me Be Lonely* 6). Ultimately, Rankine uses this material to engage large-scale existential concerns about life and death, including both individual trauma that can go unrecognized, relegated to the silence of a "personal problem," and collective trauma, such as that experienced in conjunction with the AIDS crisis in South Africa and other nations, the Gulf War, and the 9/11 attacks on the Twin Towers and other U.S. landmarks. In addition to the universal scale of existential conflicts, the poem also explores the specific precarity of Black lives brought about by interpersonal and structural racism, including hate crimes and police violence.

Given the number of different components that make up *Don't Let Me Be Lonely*, the question of how to read this book-length project is in part determined by how readers interpret the poem's form. Some of the labels critics have used, often engaging the subtitle's call to "lyric" forms, include: "a lyrical long poem" (Robbins); "vexed lyric" (Hume); "lyric sequence" (Houen); "postlyric" (Reed); "archival" (Frost, Macmillan); "collage" (Hume); "hybrid" (Robbins); "ekphrastic" (Kimberley);

and, longer descriptions such as "an experimental multi-genre project that blends poetry, essays, and images" ("Claudia Rankine Academy of American Poets"). Analyzing *Don't Let Me Be Lonely* within the lineage of social documentary forms that emerged in the 1930s, however, makes it clear that Rankine is expanding on a long tradition that allows many genres—lyric, archive, essay, image—to coexist, creating what Muriel Rukeyser calls a "third" meaning that is greater than either word or image.

Addressing how to read the conversation between images and text, Rukeyser stresses in *The Life of Poetry* (1949) that, in the combination of images and words, "there are separables: the meaning of the image, the meaning of the words, and a third, the meaning of the two in combination. The words are not used to describe the picture, but to extend its meaning" (Rukeyser 137). Rukeyser also notes how photographs can "extend the voice, / to speak this meaning" (Rukeyser, *The Collected Poems of Muriel Rukeyser* 110). Reading Rankine's poem in this tradition eliminates the falsity of choosing between competing, sometimes binary labels (lyric vs. postlyric, sequence vs. long poem) while clarifying how to interpret the ways various visual and textual elements work together on the page. Common elements of documentary poetry include narrative, description, testimony, collage, fragment, and reportage. Reading *Don't Let Me Be Lonely* in the social documentary tradition opens up avenues for understanding the relationships among different kinds of texts and various images. Parataxis is a central organizing principle of the entire poem.

The Princeton Handbook of Poetic Terms explains: "In a paratactic style, the logical relationships among elements are not specified but are left to be inferred by the reader" (Greene and Cushman). This is not to say, however, that the relationships among the various elements in *Don't Let Me Be Lonely* are random. Rather, the paratactical elements contribute to a larger field of meaning concerning mediated experience. Poet and literary critic Bob Perelman extrapolates the definition of parataxis from literature to life arguing that "[p]arataxis is the dominant mode of postindustrial experience," directing our attention to how we experience media in everyday life. Paratactic arrangement contributes to *Don't Let Me Be Lonely*'s larger themes, as the form matches and extends the content which examines the relationship of part to whole, or the individual to the larger society.

Perelman's focus on the media, and the larger themes to which the various paratactic units coming at us from the television are responding, is particularly helpful for understanding the experience of reading *Don't Let Me Be Lonely*, which metaphorically sets the reader of the book in front of the television. Perelman argues, "[a]s objects of the media, we are inundated by intense, continual bursts of narrative—twenty seconds of heart-jerk in a life insurance ad, blockbuster mini-series ten nights long—but these are tightly managed miniatures set paratactically against the conglomerate background that produces them" (Perelman 313). The concern to which *Don't Let Me Be Lonely* is responding is that focusing on the "tightly managed miniatures" diverts attention from the larger conceptual frames (conglomerate backgrounds), which are often designed to manipulate the viewer. Rankine's larger frame extends her investigation of how individual trauma is connected to collective trauma (the 9/11 attacks, endless war, institutionalized racism) which is buttressed by televised messages designed to create an emotional appeal to nationalism, corporate capitalism, patriotism, and other dominant ideologies.

Perelman, with his focus on parataxis, and scholar Emma Kimberley highlight the process of conceptual framing and settle on the need for an active reading process. "The gaps in the text force action from the reader," writes Kimberley. "The reader inhabits the interstices between the different parts of the text, and has to make choices about how to link them, in what order to read them, how to interpret them as a whole" (Kimberley 782-83). Thus, *Don't Let Me Be Lonely* represents how media can reveal information, while also concealing the mechanisms of the larger message's packaging, manipulating the viewer/reader's response, unless they are willing to do the work of active reading to uncover how that information is being framed. Analyzing pages 113-117 of *Don't Let Me Be Lonely* illustrates how parataxis functions throughout the book, engaging readers to make meaning in the "gaps" and also to trigger emotional responses.

An important characteristic of historical social documentaries is the ways they urge readers to "feel the facts" of social inequality in order to move them to action. William Stott's foundational study of social documentary in the 1930s, for example, stresses how the techniques of this genre sharpen the reportage of individual and collective histories "with feeling" to create a moving account of the effects of the Great Depression on ordinary people, while addressing the conditions that created the crisis (Stott 20). Stott explains, "Social documentary has an intellectual dimension to make clear what the facts are, why they came about, and how they can be changed for the better. Its more important dimension, however, is usually the emotional: feeling the fact may move the audience to wish to change it" (Stott 26). Placing *Don't Let Me Be Lonely* in line with this tradition thus highlights the importance of feeling, which plays a crucial role in retelling histories of historical and individual crisis.

Pages 113-117 combine lyric testimony, photographs, and listing techniques, reaching across topics from the United States' participation in wars in the Persian Gulf to stopping the spread of the HIV virus in South Africa. Page 113 consists of a long prose block that covers over half the page. On page 114, a short prose block floats above a photograph of two American flags and two hand-lettered signs. Pages 115-116 contain a list of international pharmaceutical companies, and 117 features a photograph of Nelson Mandela in the middle of the page, with two prose blocks above the photo and two below. The speaker describes a scenario which combines the mundane features of life with the urgency of life and death in times of war. People wait at a bus stop, or try to find a taxi, yet the main topic of conversation amongst the strangers they encounter is so-called "Operation Iraqi Freedom," a protracted military campaign (also known as "The Iraq War" or "The Second Persian Gulf War") which began in 2003 when the United States, Great Britain, and others invaded Iraq (113).

A long sentence makes up most of the prose block revealing many of the contradictions of this military operation and the United States' governmental rhetoric surrounding it, such as "... what is there to say since rhetorically it's not about our oil under their sand but about freeing Iraqis from Iraqis and Osama is Saddam and Saddam is 'that man who tried to kill my father' and the weapons of mass destruction, are well, invisible" (113). The U.S. offered the search for "weapons of mass destruction" in Iraq as one major justification for this war. Inspectors never found any such weapons, and thus the reference in the poem to such weapons being "invisible." Moreover, while activists against this military invasion argued, "No war for oil," the passage stresses that it is Americans' oil only "rhetorically," for the United States government seeks to maintain access to "our oil" even if it is under "their sand." Thus, the moniker "Operation Iraqi Freedom" seeks to direct attention away from the issue of the United States having access to cheap oil and gas, with the claim that the war is about "freeing" Iraqis from themselves.

A footnote at the back of the book points out that the final section on page 113—"The war in Iraq is really about peace. Trying to make the world more peaceful. This victory in Iraq, when it happens, will make the world more peaceful"—is from a statement President George W. Bush made on April 11, 2003 (152), as is presumably the quoted phrase "that man who tried to kill my father" (113), a reference to Saddam Hussein trying to kill the elder Bush and former president, George W. Bush's father. Many people thought that the younger Bush's motives for invading Iraq included avenging his father, though Americans easily mistake one Arab leader for another ("Osama is Saddam"). Thus, this passage leads readers through the twisted logic in which war equals peace. Rankine portrays such messages about Operation Iraqi Freedom as "hitting an audience already primed to be swayed by the mix of media, advertising, politics and fiction beamed into their homes 24/7" (Kimberley). The active reading needed to uncover this messaging—Bush's televised rhetoric employed to sell the Gulf War to the American public—is represented by the image of Bush as "white noise" among the static on the television, an image that the reader must also be very attentive to in order to discern.

Continuing these themes, page 114 introduces a photograph of two American flags, one with a sign below it that states "SUPPORT OUR TROOPS!" and the other with a sign blandly indicating "FOR SALE" (114). The juxtaposition of the four elements in this photograph—the two flags and the two signs—prompts the reader to question the relationships among them: What is for sale? Are the flags for sale? Is patriotism for sale? Is war a product that corporate and government interests are constantly trying to peddle to American viewers? The text accompanying the photographs on page 114 in *Don't Let Me Be Lonely* illustrates that people were quick to judge the performance of patriotism of others after the 9/11 attacks: "Nick, the super, tied a yellow ribbon but didn't do the flag thing. The distinction is not lost on anyone. The lawyer in 5B says the super should be careful he doesn't lose his job" (114). Seeking to perform the correct acts of patriotism, Americans were, Kimberley argues, "overwhelmed by the need to form a strong common identity through symbols such as the flag and the yellow ribbon" (787). A large blank space is left under the photograph on page 114, one of the gaps in which the reader can pause to consider the individual elements and their connection to the larger narratives. This section exemplifies how capitalist accumulation, buttressed through acts of violence, is masked with an invented narrative about patriotism and peace.

On the following two pages is a list beginning with the title, "THE PHARMACEUTICAL MANUFACTURERS' / ASSOCIATION OF SOUTH AFRICA," followed by the names of 39 multi-national pharmaceutical companies, alphabetized, beginning with "ALCON LABORATORIES (S.A.) / (PROPRIETARY) LIMITED (115) and ending with "WARNER-LAMBERT COMPANY" (116). The jump from the photograph of American flags to the list illustrates the use of parataxis, as well as the use of non-literary materials in the social documentary tradition. The text on the next page extends the meaning of the list, combining descriptions of mundane, everyday experience— eating breakfast while glancing at a newspaper "barely visible under the boxes of cereal, juice, and milk"—along with a larger consideration of disease, multi-national corporations, race, and power: "I see the story at first glance: President Mbeki has decided antiretrovirals will be available to the five million South Africans infected by the HIV virus" (117). The speaker informs the reader that "[b]efore Mbeki, thirty-nine drug companies filed suit in order to prevent South Africa's manufacture of AIDS drugs" (117). Thus the reader can determine the importance of the previous list: generic manufacture of the drugs within the country of South Africa would enormously decrease the profits from multinational pharmaceutical corporations' sales of their patented antiretrovirals. This is an example of how "[l]arger narrative frames, though theoretically repressed by parataxis, clearly return, even within the boundaries of a single sentence" (Perelman 321).

The pharmaceutical companies' lawsuits were eventually dropped, "But like an absurdist dream," Rankine's speaker reports, "Mbeki stood between the now available drugs and the dying" (117). Indeed, South African President Thabo Mbeki "delayed launching an antiretroviral (ARV) drug program, charging that the drugs were toxic and an effort by the West to weaken his country," a move that researchers conservatively estimate caused the premature deaths of more than 330,000 South Africans from HIV/AIDS between 2000 and 2005 (Roeder). Extending the meaning of these historical events through the combination of word and image is a photo—in the middle of page 117—of former South African President Nelson Mandela, hands raised, wearing a t-shirt that clearly reads "HIV POSITIVE" with smaller lettering below that is difficult to discern. The notes at the back of the book explain that the shirt, "was given to him by a patient at the Khayelitsha clinic" (152).

Poet and scholar Tana Jean Welch adds that this shirt was often worn by those wishing "to express solidarity with the Treatment Action Campaign (TAC), an activist group dedicated to securing HIV medications for poor South Africans" (Welch 141), which was highly influential in the 2002 Constitutional Court win for HIV treatments. "Under relentless pressure from the Treatment Action Campaign, an activist group, South Africa finally launched a program in 2003 to prevent mother-to-child transmission of HIV and a national ARV program the following year" (Roeder). Founded in 1998, TAC activists continue to "campaign and litigate on critical issues related to the quality of and access to healthcare" for users of South Africa's public healthcare system ("Our History – Timeline").

In sum, pages 113-117 of *Don't Let Me Be Lonely* illustrate how parataxis is used as a technique to enable the reader to examine Operation Iraqi Freedom, the AIDS crisis in South Africa, and affective responses to these events. Bringing these themes together, Rankine provides a framework for critiquing American exceptionalism within both a national and global context. Welch argues:

> Placing the South African antiretroviral situation within a
> discussion of the Iraq war, Rankine reframes American
> exceptionalism, suggesting that America helps other countries
> *except* when it interferes with American economic interests,
> or America cares about the life and liberty of those in other
> nations *except* the lives in Africa or the Middle East.
> (Welch 140–41)

Rankine's speaker provides a counterpoint to this ideology through her emotional responses to the news. For example, reading about South Africans being prevented from accessing life-saving medication, she notes: "It is not possible to communicate how useless, how much like a skin-sack of uselessness I felt. *I am better than thou art now. I am a fool, the fool said, though art nothing.* Is she dead? Is he dead? Yes, they are dead" (117). Here she contrasts the wise fool of *King Lear* with her perceived uselessness and concludes that she is nothing because she cannot prevent the deaths of the South Africans who will not get treatment. Moreover, this passage contributes to the book's examination of what it means to be fully "alive."

Reading the newspaper causes Rankine's speaker emotional, as well as physical, distress: "Such distress moved in with muscle and bone. Its entrance by necessity slowly translated my already grief into a tremendously exhausted hope" (118). Her empathetic response to learning that the medications will finally become available for South Africans exposes how her worries have been stored within her physical body: "My body relaxes. My shoulders fall back. I had not known that my distress at Mbeki's previous position against distribution of the drugs had physically lodged itself like a virus within me" (117). Though her grief has been transformed into a hopefulness that is labelled as "exhausted," the new hope is still affirming: "The translation occurred unconsciously, perhaps occurred simply because I am alive. Then life, which seems so full of waiting, awakes suddenly into a life of hope" (118). While much of the book considers what it means to be dead, or living with emotions such as grief, this passage illustrates that being in connection with others, through empathy, through noticing, and through social activism affirms life and creates hope.

When photographs of people are incorporated into the poem, the captioning, whether quotations attributed to the human subjects, an imagined "we" commenting on the subjects, an address to a second-person "you," or an individual lyric "I" reporting her own experience, the ethical relationship between author and subject (and thus reader and subject) is already contested. Susan Sontag contends that photographing people is a violation in and of itself (Sontag 14). In addition, "A Brief History of Photography" (1931), an essay that seems prescient in its anticipation of our current time in which people walk around with cameras in their smart phones, prepared to photograph and share everything from scenes of police brutality to banal everyday photos of what they cooked for dinner, Walter Benjamin observes that "[t]he camera will become increasingly smaller and smaller, more and more prepared to grasp fleeting, secret images whose shock will bring the mechanism of association in the viewer to a complete halt" (214). He goes on to argue, "At this point captions must begin to function, captions which understand the photography which turns all the relations of life into literature, and without which all photographic constructions must remain" (214). This statement underscores the elemental relationship between text and image as the social documentary form emerged.

Moreover, Alan Trachtenberg argues that "American photographs are not simple depictions but constructions, that the history they show is inseparable from the history they enact: a history of photographers employing their medium to make sense of their society" (xvi). *Don't Let Me Be Lonely* takes on the challenge of breaking down these processes by which history is enacted by deconstructing the framing of word and image, not just in photographs, but also in television and film. Despite the seeming straightforwardness of Trachtenberg's observation, some twenty-first century Americans still struggle to separate the subjective from the objective in an era when some elected officials encourage mistrust of factual scientific information and declare reporting that they dislike "fake news." At the same time, social media outlets have turned into engines that exacerbate existing hatreds and division through the manufacture of falsehoods masquerading as facts, including altered videos. Yet, viewers still tend to dismiss context and view photographs and other visual images uncritically, especially if the visual information appears to confirm their preexisting biases. Thus, the way in which messages—both visual and textual—are framed is crucial.

The audience's unwillingness to see conceptual frames, Kimberley asserts, "[is] seen by many American writers as the symptom of a dangerous tendency toward passive and uncritical spectatorship" (Kimberley 780). Reading Rankine alongside historical social documentaries usefully complicates how the combination of text and image can bring to bear differing relations between the reader/viewer and the subjects being documented. Actively reading and analyzing these relationships is necessary for social documentary's purported purpose of conveying meaning that causes the reader to "feel," rather than only learn, the facts of the case under investigation. Rankine sharpens individual and collective histories with feeling, which also highlights the ethical relationship between self and other. Rankine creates what I am terming an archive of feeling that extends the document even further.

Highlighting how the speaker's responses are both intellectual and affective, *Don't Let Me Be Lonely* also brings what are often perceived to be individual, private feelings—sadness, pain, depression, grief, hope—into the historical record to create the archive of feeling. An important effect of this practice, as scholar Rebecca Macmillan argues, is that *Don't Let Me Be Lonely* "…contests the faulty conception that 'sad' connotes something feeble" or "something that may be casually left behind in the instant it takes to switch TV channels" (195). Thus, unlike some previous examples of social documentary, *Don't Let Me Be Lonely* expands the archive to include forms of personal documentation. One such example is a photograph of an ailing friend and his message scratched into a slate message board—"THIS IS THE MOST / MISERABLE IN MY LIFE" (17)—as he attempts to cope with the effects of Alzheimer's.

The photograph of the message on the board appears twice on page 17, interrupted by text, and twice again on page 18. The last time the image appears, it is connected to another photograph, partially revealing an aging man's face and hand (18). The first-person speaker relates: "For a while he understands he is getting ill and will die within this illness" (17). This is the period in which he permanently scratches the message "with some sort of sharp edge" into the chalkboard's surface, though it "has a built-in ledge, on the ledge is an eraser" (18). Although his illness is causing his memory, and his life, to be impaired, the man's feelings of misery form a kind of permanent record that cannot be erased, and the speaker collects it after his death. "I bring the chalkboard home with me and hang it on the wall in my study. Whenever I look up from my desk it is there—" (17). This is an example of what the speakers in the book do in order not to abandon one another, not to let each other be lonely. The speaker stays with her ailing friend and preserves the chalkboard, a human document, which shows he was not left alone in his suffering, nor is he "erased" after his death.

Macmillan argues that *Don't Let Me Be Lonely* "showcases personal effects as significant forms of documentation, affirming the need to uncover and examine the connections between what appears at first to be solely individual and those broader, structural contemporary conditions" (189). This is a hallmark of Rankine's works that examine individual experiences within larger social frameworks; for example, illness is not just a personal problem or individual failure but, rather, is impacted by a variety of social institutions that impede or grant access to essentials for living such as healthcare, nutritious food, a clean environment, and safety when interacting with police. In addition, while government statistics collect a history of the incidence of Alzheimer's, the friend's message—both "sharp" in its making and sharp in the fear that it produces of being "on the ledge" as if ready to jump or fall—form another kind of history, an archive of feeling enabled because a friend is present to be with him in his anguish and also to preserve the record of it. Rankine thus pushes these questions forward to consider the ethics of the relationship between the self and others: "Why are we here if not for each other?" (62).

Rankine's archive of feeling builds upon Muriel Rukeyser's theories in *The Life of Poetry* (1949) that argue that poetry can engage the intellect but must do so by first engaging the emotions, which is evident in Rukeyser's documentary poem "The Book of the Dead" from *U.S. 1* (1938), which addresses the deaths of miners in West Virginia. For Rukeyser, this ability to reach readers both affectively (through what "Public Feelings" scholar Ann Cvetkovich labels "sensation and feeling") and intellectually is one marker of a good poem. "This response is total, but it is reached through the emotions. A fine poem will seize your imagination intellectually—that is, when you reach it, you will reach it intellectually too—but the way is through emotion, through what we call feeling" (Rukeyser 8). Though Rukeyser does archive individual feelings in "The Book of the Dead," for example, through the inclusion of witness testimony, Rankine expands the reach of her archive to include personal ephemera, such as a prescription label, which is considered private, part of one's medical records, but not a public document.

Rankine uses these personal items to document private feelings. Like the historical social documentary tradition (but differing in the kind of media images it collects) *Don't Let Me Be Lonely* also combines text and image to produce an affective response to social inequality.

Stott writes, "We understand a historical document intellectually, but we understand a human document emotionally. In the second kind of document, as in documentary and thirties documentary as a whole, feeling comes first" (Stott 8). What Stott calls a "human document" is central to *Don't Let Me Be Lonely*; employing this kind of documentation allows Rankine to engage history by creating not only an archive of historical events, but also an archive of feeling. Therefore, as scholar Rebecca Macmillan argues, "ordinary feelings" rise to a place of importance: "[*Don't Let Me Be Lonely*] compels consideration of how the past gets represented, referenced, and made sense of—and how history conditions and resides in the present, even at the level of ordinary feelings" (Macmillan 189). This approach expands the consideration of what constitutes history, adjusting the scale of what is considered worth recording to include the individual, experiential, and affective. As Cvetkovich argues, "...the focus on sensation and feeling as the register of historical experience gives rise to new forms of documentation and writing..." (Cvetkovich 11). Though Cvetkovich is not writing about Rankine specifically, her argument opens ways for understanding how *Don't Let Me Be Lonely* creates new forms of documentation to archive affective historical experiences.

Historically, the practice of combining text and image in documentary poetry can be traced to the emerging genres of documentary photography and documentary film in the 1930s, and collaborations between authors and photographers in the form of the magazine photo essay and the collaborative photo-book. Stott explains that a now familiar form, the photo essay (published in Henry Luce's magazines, including *Time*, *Life* and

Fortune), was a particularly important antecedent of the photo-book collaborations, as was *Fortune* magazine's mid-thirties "Life and Circumstances" series, with wonderfully descriptive feature stories such as "Success Story: The Life and Circumstances of Mr. Gerald Corkum, Paint Sprayman at the Plymouth Motor Plant" (Stott 211).

Following on the photo-essay, entire books combining text with photographs documenting the effects of the Great Depression were published. Two well-known examples of these Depression-era collaborative photo-books are photographer Margaret Bourke-White's and novelist Erskine Caldwell's *You Have Seen Their Faces* (1937), which uses text, photographs, and captions to document the lives of Southern tenant farmers, and *An American Exodus: A Record of Human Erosion* (1939), by photographer Dorothea Lange and her husband economist Paul Schuster Taylor (Lange and Taylor), who documented rural poverty and westward mass migration for the Farms Securities Administration (FSA).

A different approach to this subject is evident in Richard Wright's *12 Million Black Voices: A Folk History of the Negro in the United States* (1941), which combines Wright's text with FSA photographs selected by Edwin Rosskam depicting the effects of the Great Depression on African Americans, and Archibald MacLeish's *Land of the Free* (1938). *Land of the Free* is a book-length poem that brings together documentary photographs (verso) and "poetic social comment" (recto). Finally, of the notable precursors, Rankine's documentary style has a particular kinship with Rukeyser's documentary poem "The Book of the Dead" from *U.S. 1* (1938), which contains no photographs at all (though Rukeyser had intended to use them). Instead, the book contains documents that Rukeyser assembled while conducting research about the Gauley Bridge tragedy in West Virginia that appears in the poem itself, including newspaper articles, witness testimonies, court transcripts, and a stock ticker that illustrates that Union Carbide's main concern was profits, not worker safety. Hundreds of miners, primarily African Americans, who had not been issued protective equipment by parent company Union Carbide, developed a painful and deadly disease called silicosis after blasting rock for a tunnel. Unknown to the workers, the rock was filled with silicates—fine, glass-like particles—that they had inhaled into their lungs.

"While we've come a long way in realizing the limits or impossibility of 'objective' documentation," poet and scholar Susan Briante argues, "the desire to investigate, the need for facts, images, and documents seems even more pressing" (Briante). Indeed, Rankine, like Rukeyser before her, employed research and documentation in the process of writing this book, noting that *"Don't Let Me Be Lonely* is a book full of research, ... [that] was really the bringing together of a lot of newspaper articles, transcripts, legal documents . . . all of that. That was me working with documents" (Rankine, "The History Behind the Feeling"). Rankine uses the images in conjunction with the text to document current events and social injustices, such as the brutalizing of Black men, including the murder of James Byrd, the police attack on Abner Louima, and the murder of Amadou Diallo, also by police. Asked how she came to include such source materials and images in her work, Rankine explains that "the introduction of images in *Don't Let Me Be Lonely* was an attempt to acknowledge a total experience of being—to involve as many of our senses as possible" (Rankine, "Poetry Daily Prose Feature: Interview with Claudia Rankine"). This is how the various source materials made their way into the poem: not decided in advance, but encountered through Rankine's daily life, her "experience of being."

Reflecting on what images she chose to include in *Don't Let Me Be Lonely*, Rankine explains: "At first I thought I would only bring back people who needed to be brought back in images—in most cases it ended up being black men, like Abner Louima. But then I realized other parts of the project could be served by a conversation set up through the text's relation to the image" (Rankine, "Poetry Daily Prose Feature: Interview with Claudia Rankine"). In addition to being a documentary poem, *Don't Let Me Be Lonely*, therefore, is a collective account, "An American Lyric," which is also a chronicle of its maker, presented through the speaker's accounts of her affective responses to the news.

As the format of the photo-book became popular, opinion was divided as to how to integrate the textual and visual components. For example, social documentary filmmaker and film advisor to the U.S. Resettlement Administration, Pare Lorentz, who admired Lange's photographs, "criticised the organisation of *An American Exodus* for its spatial integration of diverse materials (which included clippings from newspapers, maps, and quotations from agricultural magazines)" (Gander 26). Lorentz argued that the photographs should be displayed in a separate section to highlight their importance. Yet, Lange's and Taylor's intention was that all elements—photographs, captions, and text—remain equal (Gander 26). This is also an important consideration for *Don't Let Me Be Lonely*, which places image and text in diverse combinations without the expectation that one has be used to explain the other. Rankine's combination of photos and a first-person speakerly voice enacts the role of reportage, reporting facts, while also presenting the speaker's physical and emotional responses to those facts.

Archibald MacLeish came to social documentary through several avenues, including his work for *Fortune* magazine throughout the 1930s and his active involvement in public life. Despite the recognition he garnered for his poetry during his lifetime (he won the Pulitzer Prize, a National Book Award, and a Bollingen Prize) MacLeish's *Land of the Free* is now mostly forgotten. It includes 88 photographs representing scenes from throughout the country, such as "Oklahoma drought refuges in California, Tennessee coal-miner migrants, Iowa farmers, Dakota sod houses, Mississippi cotton sharecroppers, now landless; a farmhouse in Indiana after flood; erosion in Alabama" (Jack). On the back jacket flap, MacLeish describes it as "a book of photographs illustrated by a poem" (rather than "a book of poems illustrated by photographs"). Not a collaborative project, MacLeish was taking up a challenge to make creative use of the photographs on his own. As in the emerging tradition of documentary film, MacLeish also conceived of the poem as a "soundtrack" for the photos, and, similar to Rukeyser, MacLeish argued for the importance of poetry as a vehicle for both thinking and feeling: "Unless poetry can not only perceive, but also feel, the race of men to be more important than any one man, we are merely fighting back against the water. . . . It is no longer A MAN against the stars. It is Mankind" (MacLeish 57) Opinions are divided as to how successfully MacLeish was able to produce a work that enacted this ideology.

Rukeyser, at the time of the book's publication, remarked upon the "great lack of balance" in MacLeish's *Land of the Free* and bemoaned that the poem "often falls into loosenesses and sentimentalities" (Rukeyser, "'We Aren't Sure...We're Wondering'" 27). Rukeyser felt that the poem distances the reader from the subjects in the photographs, so much so that she describes it as being "in somebody else's mouth" (27). To do justice to the people in the photographs, Rukeyser calls on the poet "to supply the cleanest, sharpest most alive words we know to meet these faces and these scenes" (28). The verb "meet" indicates an equal relationship between word and image.

Her emphasis on the "third meaning" also puts the elements on the page into motion, leading Rukeyser to seek out a new kind of expression: "Here we need something like a poem, something like movie titles, something like news in lights around the Times building" (27). Rukeyser's "Book of the Dead," like

Lange's and Taylor's *An American Exodus*, thus seeks to present images and words as equal in significance (the words do not explain the images or vice versa) generating a new art form where the combination of the two present new meanings for an age in which news circles a building in electrical lights, "extending the document," and putting it into motion. This is the same ideology Rankine employs in *Don't Let Me Be Lonely*, actually extending the document even further, from news expressed in electric lights to news presented on television.

Scholar Catherine Gander explains: "The poem therefore must not rely on the photographs for message, or movement, but, through a meeting of textual forms and styles collaborate with the images to create a new, communicative art form" (31). Rukeyser's experience working in journalism and cinema, Gander shows, contributed to Rukeyser's "developing sensibility within her writing towards a relational poetics that sought to connect ostensibly separate fields" (Gander 31). This is an important formal aspect of documentary poetry that includes visual images and written forms considered "non-literary" such as Rukeyser's stock ticker and transcripts of Congressional testimonies and Rankine's photograph of a stack of wooden stretchers not needed at the World Trade Center site after the attack (82) and a transcription of a conversation with a taxi driver (89-90).

These early examples of documentary illustrate how forms of media, including the news (print journalism) and visual media (photography and cinema) influence the development of new poetic forms. Rankine even created a visual design for the poem that would mimic the layout of a newspaper. In addition, Rankine works collaboratively with documentary photographer and filmmaker John Lucas, fashioning a relationship between text and image approaching that in the collaborative work of Lange and Taylor.

In her work on "Public Feelings" and affect, Cvetkovich reminds us, however, that "[t]he documentation of everyday life is not an end in itself." (11). She goes on to explain: "The richer accounts of the ordinary sought by the Public Feelings projects are also new ways of providing the more systemic accounts of power that have been central to cultural studies. Depression, or alternative accounts of what gets called depression, is thus a way to describe neoliberalism and globalization, or the current state of political economy, in affective terms" (Cvetkovich 11). Anti-depressants and the commercial interests of the multi-national pharmaceutical industry are particular targets in *Don't Let Me Be Lonely*.

For example, a slogan that appears in a commercial for the drug Paxil, "YOUR LIFE IS WAITING," flashes across the television screen inserted near the bottom of the page 29, and later as an afterimage when the speaker closes her eyes "to check if I am sleeping" (29). This passage prompts the reader to consider if one is ever fully awake, conscious, during the experience of consuming television. Television delivers information to our living rooms, but that information has already been interpreted for us, framed to produce the feelings and desires that the creators wish to impose upon viewers. Through what Kevin Bell calls "the uninterrupted 24-hour drone of consumerist noise" (101), television sells us a version of happiness and shows us which products to buy to obtain it. The speaker reports: "One commercial for PAXIL (paroxetine HCI) says simply, YOUR LIFE IS WAITING. Parataxis, I think first, but then I wonder, for what, for what does it wait. For life I guess" (29). The speaker wonders what the relationship of this slogan is to the drug being advertised, and to her own life, finally asking: for what does her life wait? If her life is waiting for life, is she in fact alive?

Death lingers on the edges of childhood, but is not seen or spoken of. The speaker's pregnant mother returns from the hospital without a baby—"Where's the baby? we asked. Did she shrug"?—and the speaker's father leaves to attend his own mother's funeral: "When he returned he spoke neither of the airplane or the funeral" (5). Death remains invisible, outside the edges of the frame, made all the more unreal by its representation in television and movies. This leads the speaker to deeper self-questioning, "Or one begins asking oneself that same question differently: Am I dead?" (7). The confusion or slippage between the states of being alive and being dead in *Don't Let Me Be Lonely* reveal a continuous state of trauma. Theorist Cathy Caruth asks, "Is the trauma the encounter with death, or the ongoing experience of having survived it?" suggesting at the core of trauma narratives is a "double telling," which she describes as "the oscillation between a *crisis of death* and the correlative *crisis of life*: between the story of the unbearable nature of an event and the story of the unbearable nature of its survival" (Caruth 7). Thus, wondering "am I dead?" leads to the corollary, but ultimately different, question: "Am I alive?" And, what does it mean to be alive if life is a continual state of crisis?

Kevin Bell argues that television creates a "externally programmed fantasy of agency…" (102). Thus, "… there is no collectivity, no partnership, but only the administration and projection of 'life' on camera that the spectator passively (mis)takes for his or her own" (K. Bell 102). Rankine's various speakers look to televised images to affirm life and death. At the book's outset, death is unreal, experienced only through images onscreen: "The years went by and people only died on television…" (5). However, the young speaker sees that death is associated with blackness, noting of the people dying on television, "—if they weren't Black, they were wearing black or were terminally ill" (5), suggesting that images of Black people dying on television are more predominant.

The speaker attempts to connect death onscreen with death in real life, recalling, "Every movie I saw in the third grade compelled me to ask, Is he dead? Is she dead? Because the characters often live against all odds it is the actors whose mortality concerned me" (6). The speaker tries to connect fiction with reality, but there is still confusion about who is actually alive. She reports that "[i]f it were an old black-and-white film" whoever was around would respond that the actor was in fact dead. Yet, when the actor appears months later "on some late-night talk show to promote his latest efforts," the speaker points out, "You said he was dead. And the misinformed would claim, I never said he was dead" (6).

As the speaker lies awake at night, pondering life and death, she considers the perniciousness of commercials: "It seems right that pharmaceutical companies should advertise in the middle of the night, when people are less distracted and capable of tuning in more and more and most precisely to their fearful bodies and their accompanying anxieties" (29). In the middle of the night insomniacs are able to "tune in" to more and more television, which directs their fearful wakefulness to the exact product that can cure their anxieties. The company's drugs, the commercial tell us, can provide the viewer with the "life" for which they are presumably "waiting" as the night passes. Moreover, lying prone in the dark, wavering on the edge of sleep, highlights the passive experience of consuming television images. It also suggests a coffin-like posture, figuring the TV viewer as "dead" unless they are willing to use this particular medication.

A conversation about what it means to *think* one is dead or to *feel* dead is presented as a dialogue in the margin of a notebook:

I thought I was dead.
You thought you were dead?
I thought I was.
Did you feel dead?
I said, God rest me.

God rest your soul?
I thought I was dead. (16)

The concerns center around thinking, feeling, and the sacred. The dialogue concludes with the following two lines around which the book centers: "You'd let me be lonely? / I thought I was dead" (16). Throughout the poem, the various subjects seek *not* to be lonely, which figures being alive as having a responsibility to be present for the other.

The television static, on the other hand, symbolizes interruption, breaks in attention, and the static overload of information playing on the many screens surrounding us at the beginning of the twenty-first century. The black-and-white static, or what Bell notes is "… the random black-and-white dot pattern generally referred to as television 'snow'" (K. Bell 93), both interrupts and fails to cease. While the sudden intrusion of the sight and sound of television "snow" jarringly interrupts one's scheduled programming, it continues its loud, staticky intrusion long after one has changed the channel because there is always another screen to take its place. The snow obscures any possible communication, both visually and aurally, but the television itself already serves as an intermediary between the subject/viewer and the attempted communication being transmitted through the machine. The technology of television, like the technology of writing, is always in danger of missing its intended audience, of failing to communicate. Whether or not the audience is present, the machine drones on: "I leave the television on all the time. It faces the empty bed" (15). Literary critic Amy Moorman Robbins argues that the book reveals how "…language always falls short of communicating to another the essential loneliness of the autonomous American individual in a profoundly alienating media-saturated culture" (140). We may feel that we are together, watching the same shows and commercials, purchasing the same products, but we are alone.

As Robbins argues, Rankine's speakers meditate on the theme of death as both "... literal and metaphorical, private and visually spectacular (as in 'televised')" (Robbins 140). Rankine considers how Black life and death are televised, for example, with images of a somber Abner Louima flanked by lawyers (56) and a relaxed Amadou Diallo smiling for a candid photo before his death (57), placed within the boundaries of television screen, like a frame. Beneath the photo of Louima, the speaker reminds the reader of the brutal facts: "It's been four years since he was sodomized with a broken broomstick while in police custody. It was two months and three surgeries before he could leave the hospital" (56). Significantly, the speaker feels physical pain when she sees Louima's face on the television: "Sometimes I look into someone's face and I must brace myself—the blow on its way" (56). When a reporter asks Louima, who has reached a monetary settlement with the city and the police union, how it feels to be rich, he responds, "Not rich, says Louima. Lucky, lucky to be alive."

As he says these words, the speaker considers the pain that Louima suffers and she also feels pain, instinctively bracing her abdomen for "the sharp pain in my gut" and "a feeling of bits of my inside twisting away from flesh in the form of a blow to the body" (56). Robbins writes, "The poem's many and varied meditations on the politics of death, grief, and mourning are folded into a narrative that includes the speaker's quest to understand her own particular place as a racialized citizen in the twenty-first century" (Robbins), which includes both emotional and physical pain. This meditation explores the ways that pain and loss are represented and also felt by the speaker in the poem who is viewing the images. The speaker's response to Louima's pain highlights how affective responses can generate ethical relationships between self and other through empathy.

A passage from philosopher Emmanuel Levinas's "The Transcendence of Words" (1949) concerning the relationship of the subject to the other is one of the collaged materials included in *Don't Let Me Be Lonely*:

> The subject who speaks is situated in relation to the other. This privilege of the other ceases to be incomprehensible once we admit that the first fact of existence is neither being in itself nor being for itself but being for the other, in other words, that human existence is a creature. By offering a word, the subject putting himself forward lays himself open, and in a sense, prays. (Rankine 120)

"Being for the other" creates a connection that will mitigate loneliness. Not only is the relationship between the self and the other sacred, but the offering of words to the other is sacred. This duty places the poet in the role of creating a sacred contract between the poem and its readers: offering words, laying themselves open, is the poet's act of prayer. Alex Houen notes that "… for Levinas, because a person is riven with otherness, speaking is always a matter of declaring 'for everyone and everything'—though his ethical emphasis is on other *people* more than anything else" (Houen 242). *Don't Let Me Be Lonely* offers this ethical emphasis as a marker of being alive, being present for others.

Through capturing the reader's affective responses in the mode of social documentary, responses that readers also witness in the speakers of the poem, the process of reading *Don't Let Me Be Lonely* leads to intellectual, in addition to emotional, considerations, of the ethical questions surrounding the relationship between self and other. Rankine concludes with quotations from poet Paul Celan, who compared the poem to a handshake, as her speaker underscores the need to be present for one another. Above a photograph of a billboard that simply states: "HERE.", the speaker concludes, "Hence the poem is that—Here. I am here" (130). The conclusion is a response to the first billboard we see on the book's cover which states, "DON'T LET ME BE LONELY." Being "here" is to be present for the other: "We must both be here in this world in this life in this place indicating the presence of," Rankine writes, "or in other words, I am here" (131). The poem is the that connection between self and other, through word and image, that brings the reader to being together, here.

5

Remaking the Social Body in *Citizen*

Claudia Rankine's most well-known book, *Citizen: An American Lyric* (2014), is arranged into six numbered sections, or "chapters," of mostly prose poems interspersed with a variety of visual images including photographs, screengrabs from internet and television sources, and full-color reproductions of selected pieces of contemporary art. *Citizen* continues *Don't Let Me Be Lonely*'s documentary form, combining text and image to enlarge the meaning of the poem. With *Citizen*, however, Rankine intentionally sought to engage with public conversations about race. In a collection of vignettes throughout the book, Rankine details everyday actions of racism (sometimes called "microaggressions," though their effects are not small) that occur in interpersonal encounters. While it may be easier to talk about discrimination on a macro level, it can be uncomfortable for some, and extremely painful to others, to face how racism plays out in one's own social interactions, which is part of what *Citizen* is asking of its readers. In a 2014 interview, Rankine notes how the book engages public discussion (the social) and feelings as well as thought (affect): "It felt like the first time I could actively be involved in a public discussion about race, in a discussion that, to me, is essential to our well-being as a country. ... It was also an opportunity for me to learn what others really thought and felt" (Lee). The expression of private feelings about interactions that go unremarked is central not only to the health of the individual body, but also to the social body. As *Citizen* stresses, "What feels more than feeling?" (152).

Each of the incidents included in the poem occurred in the lives of people Rankine spoke with, or she experienced them herself. In an interview conducted in 2015, Rankine explained to

NPR's Eric Westervelt that "all of the encounters described in her book actually happened." Rankine continues, "There's no imagination, actually. Many of the anecdotes in the book were gathered by asking friends of mine to tell me moments when racism surprisingly entered in when you were among friends or colleagues, or just doing some ordinary thing in your day" (Westervelt). Thus, *Citizen* tracks individual feelings within social relations structured by racial hierarchies, the racist evaluations and assumptions that suddenly arise within social relations presumed to be neutral (standing in line in a store) or even intimate (a long-term friendship).

These fractures of the social body occur in the space between what Rankine calls the "historical self" and the "self-self" in Section I:

A friend argues that Americans battle between the "historical self" and the "self-self." By this she means you mostly interact as friends with mutual interest and, for the most part, compatible personalities; however, sometimes your historical selves, her white self and your black self, or your white self and her black self, arrive with the full force of your American positioning. (14)

History impacts the construction of the self even as one assumes herself to be a discrete individual having private experiences unrelated to a historical continuum. However, as *Citizen* demonstrates, the intimate attachments of the "self self" become "fragile, tenuous" when transgressed within the social body made up of historical selves (14). Rankine's invocations of the social, along with an attention to intimacy and affect, urge readers to contemplate how the social body might be redrawn in a way that fully appreciates the humanity of each person, bringing together the art of poetry with the art of social change, a change that must first occur within the imagination.

This chapter presents three unique formal features of *Citizen* that contribute to the poem's engagement with the social, both the personal interactions that Rankine describes in the interview above and the social body made up of larger groups and institutions. These formal elements include the use of the second person "you" (rather than a lyric "I"), and the poem scripts and videos that make up Rankine's video poem collaborations with John Lucas, as well as the incorporation of other visual images in the text. The eight scripts in Section VI for the "Situation" video poems on which Rankine and Lucas collaborated are "August 29, 2005 / Hurricane Katrina" (82-87); "February 26, 2012 / In Memory of Trayvon Martin" (88-91); "June 26, 2011 / In Memory of James Craig Anderson" (92-97); "December 4, 2006 / Jena Six" (98-103); "Stop-and-Frisk" (104-113); "August 4, 2011 / In Memory of Mark Duggan" (114-119); "October 10, 2006 / World Cup" (120-129); and "July 29—August 18, 2014 / Making Room: Script for Public Fiction at Hammer Museum" (130-133). In noting these pages, I am including both the texts for the scripts, as well as the visual elements printed within them. Though the works in the book are labeled as "scripts," the poems, in the form of Rankine's voiceover, that are recorded as soundtracks to the videos, often differ from the poems in the book. I thus distinguish the printed poems from what I am calling video poems. The video poems, "Stop-and-Frisk," and "August 29, 2005 / Hurricane Katrina," are analyzed extensively.

The images discussed in this chapter include a historical photograph, "Public Lynching," taken on August 30, 1930. Rankine also uses full-color reproductions of contemporary art in the book to further highlight the ongoing history of Black people being seen as nonhuman, linking the historical photo with contemporary artwork. The images are of pieces by artists including Kate Clark, Nick Cave, Glenn Ligon, Mel Chin, Toyin Odutola, John Lucas, Carrie Mae Weems, Radcliffe Bailey,

Wangechi Mutu, and Joseph Mallford William Turner. The images discussed are Glenn Ligon's *Untitled (Speech/Crowd) #2* (2000) and *Untitled: Four Etchings* (1992); a sculpture, *Little Girl*, by Kate Clark (2008); and a panel from a mixed media collage, *Sleeping Heads*, by Mangechi Mutu (2006). The images are untitled within the text and create an interesting interruption, causing the reader to pause and reflect. (Titles, medium, and credits for each work are listed at the back of the book.) "While the images themselves are disturbing, they belong to an elite world of museums, galleries, and private collections. They are exquisitely made and pleasurable even in their disturbances" says Rankine (Rankine, "Interview by Lauren Berlant"). Pausing and sitting with images allows the reader to reflect on the disturbing questions that the artwork raises.

Asked why she chose to write about racism in such a personal way, Rankine explains, "I wanted to create the field of the encounter; what happens when one body comes up against another and race enters into the moment of intimacy between two people" (Westervelt). Rankine's interest in actual and metaphorical points of social contact, what scholar Nikki Skillman describes as "the physical touch of recognition and the contact the poem facilitates between writing and reading subjects that are in fact, in most cases, inexorably separated by time and space," can be traced to Rankine's previous book, *Don't Let Me Be Lonely* (2004), the first of her "American Lyric" installments, in which Rankine refers to Paul Celan's statement comparing a poem to a handshake. The poem, then, reaches across time to connect disparate individuals. Rankine writes, "This conflation of the solidity of presence with the offering of this same presence perhaps has everything to do with being alive" (Rankine, *Don't Let Me Be Lonely* 130). The marker of aliveness is to be present for others. In *Citizen*, Rankine takes this concern with the assertion "I am here" a step further within moments of contact and recognition, as she engages not only presence but also the effacement produced by racialized structures and encounters.

For example, the hand that extends in *Citizen*, "fighting off the weight / of nonexistence," is not recognized or received by the other.

> And still this life parts your lids, you see
> you seeing your extending hand
>
> as a falling wave—
>
> I they he she we you turn
> only to discover
> the encounter
>
> to be alien to this place.
>
> Wait. (139-140)

The action of the wave cannot be completed; it falls, as "you" discover this "encounter"—this potential point of contact—to be "alien." In fact, the hand itself is alien, disconnected from "you" as you watch it extending ("you see / you") and falling as if watching an alien appendage. The "solidity of presence" is deferred. In much of *Citizen*, "you" must wait, pause, sigh. The "presence perhaps [that] has everything to do with being alive" is precarious, as Black bodies risk being wasted in death. This precariousness begins in the field of encounter.

Though *Citizen* is not singularly autobiographical, Rankine does note how the book reflects her own identities and experiences. "I made a conscious decision to inhabit my own subjectivity in this book in the sense that the middle-class life I live, with my highly educated, professional, and privileged friends, remains as the backdrop for whatever is being foregrounded," Rankine explains to scholar Lauren Berlant.

"Everyone is having a good time together—doing what they do, buying what they can afford, going where they go—until they are not. The break in the encounter wouldn't wound without the presumed intimacy and the good times" (Rankine, "Interview by Lauren Berlant"). Such intimate portrayals also work against perceptions of the separation of different races, of white's impressions of Black life occurring in an unacknowledged zone elsewhere, by presenting examples of what is really happening in shared social spaces (Rankine's "field of the encounter") as well as portraying a multiplicity of Black identities.

For example, in one vignette, the speaker describes attending an event to hear an author talk about his new book: "Someone in the audience asks the man promoting his new book on humor what makes something funny. His answer is what you expect—context" (48). At this point, the field of encounter is "what you expect" and "you" are included as part of the audience, not as separate from the group. However, "After a pause he adds that if someone said something, like about someone, and you were with your friends you would probably laugh, but if they said it out in public where black people could hear what was said, you might not, probably would not," (48) and this is the where the rupture occurs—as "race happens." White people are "friends"; Black people are "others." "Only then do you realize that you are among 'the others out in public' and not among 'friends'" (48). The Black audience member is cast out of the group of "friends" with this statement, whereas before she felt included in an audience of people who would attend this kind of presentation. The word "context" is also key: the Black audience member is removed from her spot inside the context of a shared experience and placed outside with "the others" who do not find anything funny in this statement.

One of Rankine's formal strategies to draw together a wide variety of readers into such points of contact is implicating them through the use of the second person. Skillman argues that the use of the second person to address the reader directly has a long history and is employed by a wide variety of poets such as John Keats, Walt Whitman, and John Ashbery (Skillman 438). For Rankine, however, its use uniquely illustrates the often ignored, or unspoken, relations of racial inequality. Paula Cocozza, writing for *The Guardian* in 2015, explains how Rankine arrived at the idea to present the work using the second person "you": "She started writing it in the first person, but could not make it work: the stories belonged to other people, too. When she hit on the idea of the second person, initially it was a 'joke'—about blackness as the second person, she says" (Cocozza). Race (blackness) is the second, unacknowledged person in the room.

Being addressed as "you," involves, connects, even incriminates the readers of *Citizen*. For example, poet Erica Hunt contends that "[t]he word 'you,' contains volumes of nuance" and can project tones that are variously "commanding, accusative, or adoring" (Hunt). Hunt elaborates: "These uses of 'you' compass multiple points of reference, at times denoting an internal 'you' — the 'you' of self-talk and admonition — and at other times, the performing 'you,' as if spoken by a stage director guiding an enactment of the social self" (Hunt). This becomes further evident in the version of *Citizen* adapted for the stage, called *Citizen Affirmed*, which highlights the realm of the social and our relationships with one another. Dramatizing the narratives for the stage, however, may lessen the impact that the second-person "you" has on the page, where the reader can locate the shifting referents as "you" is repeated.

Furthermore, by beginning the book with close personal interactions, Rankine swiftly draws readers from various subject positions (including gender, race, and class) into the narratives, some of which they may personally recognize, having experienced, perpetrated, or witnessed similar exchanges themselves. Thus,

Citizen's "you" refuses to denote a single addressee, let alone one gender or one racial identity. Its referent changes from line to line. It telescopes in and out, singularises, pluralises, reverses, and its shifts keep the reader mobile, continually asking: Which one am I? Where do I fit in? It is impossible to read without questioning your own part in the racist social structures it recounts. (Cocozza)

Moreover, because "you" can also be plural, Rankine switches from lyric individuality to collective relationality. Thus, she matches the form with the content that encourages readers to consider themselves within the context of the social, rather simply as individuals.

Hunt adds that the address "you" "rotates," so that it is sometimes "facing inward and sometimes outward." This may prompt white readers to consider moments when they have failed to recognize Black people, even friends, as individuals, just as the woman who sometimes confuses her friend with her housekeeper in Section I. Here an adult speaker describes "a close friend who early in your friendship, when distracted, would call you by the name of her black housekeeper" and, "You assumed you two were the only black people in her life" (7). The speaker asks, "Do you feel hurt because it's the 'all black people look the same' moment, or because you are being confused with another after being so close to the other?" (7). This is an example of the "rotating" "you." In the sentence beginning, "You assumed," "you" (the pronoun) might be directed inwardly (the speaker addressing herself), or outwardly (addressing another, or Black people as a group).

Moreover, while the question "Do you feel hurt . . . ?" might be posed to a single individual, it might address Black citizens collectively, also. Such interactions between Black and white friends may remain unacknowledged, this interaction shows us, but can nonetheless alter the relationship forever, piercing the bonds of trust and intimacy: "And you never called her on it (why not?) and yet, you don't forget. If this were a domestic tragedy, and it might well be, this would be your fatal flaw—your memory, vessel of your feelings" (7). What is here named the "fatal flaw" is also the foundation on which the stakes of *Citizen* are laid: affect, the "vessel of your feelings." Even as Black citizens in everyday life are exhorted to "move on" and not challenge racist social structures, the memories of traumatic interactions remain.

Writing for the *New York Times* in 2014, Felicia R. Lee reports some of the different responses Rankine has received from readers of *Citizen*:

> Ms. Rankine said she was hearing from black readers who feel comforted that she understands their exhaustion of being rendered invisible or alien, even when they believe they have forged connections in spite of race. And she is hearing from white readers who say they are more conscious of how their race determines their behavior and controls their imagination.

This reflection is enabled throughout *Citizen* as such moments accumulate in everyday interactions, including in close relationships, when "race happens." Whether intentionally or unintentionally, the white person inflicts harm on the black or brown person, and the interpersonal relationship is damaged: "And when the woman with the multiple degrees says, I didn't know black women could get cancer, instinctively you take two steps back though all urgency leaves the possibility of any kind of relationship as you realize nowhere is where you will get from here" (45). The gulf of misunderstanding is so wide here—a supposedly well-educated white woman with "multiple degrees" failing to grasp that Black women inhabit the same human bodies as other women and are subject to the same diseases—that the speaker withdraws, in shock and for safety, realizing she is going to get nowhere in trying to pursue the relationship further.

Contemporary art further emphasizes this dehumanization. Kate Clark, whose work is reproduced on page 19 of *Citizen*, uses taxidermy to create sculptures that merge animal and human forms, creating pieces of art that are not only difficult to look at, but also hard to turn away from. "A traditional taxidermist will tan the animal's hide, removing the flesh and cartilage to preserve the skin and fur, before draping it around a foam body made to look like the animal in real life. But artist Kate Clark does things differently," explains filmmaker Kathryn Carlson.

> Instead of fresh hides, she recycles old ones that are considered imperfect for the typical purposes of trophy mounts. Whether they were left too long in the freezer or bugs ate holes in the skin, she will stitch them together with care, before lopping off the foam animal head and replacing it with one made of clay, sculpted to have human features and then covered in the animal's own facial skin. (Carlson)

Clark's sculpture, *Little Girl* (2008), is particularly arresting. *Little Girl* features an image of a Black girl's face attached to a deer-like body constructed of "infant caribou hide, foam, clay, pins, thread [and] rubber eyes" (Rankine, *Citizen* 163).

Viewers of Clark's sculptures express different reactions, ranging from disgust and horror to contemplation of how humans have separated themselves so completely from the natural world that we no longer have good knowledge of that world. For example, most viewers do not notice that Clark has attached female faces to some animals sporting antlers, "an appendage usually sported only by male animals" (Carlson). For Rankine, the sculpture *Little Girl* reaches into the history of Africans first brought to the Americas as slaves who were not considered human. Rankine explains, "[Clark] attached the black girl's face on this deer-like body—it says it's an infant caribou in the caption—and I was transfixed by the memory that my historical body on this continent began as property no different from an animal. It was a thing hunted and the hunting continues on a certain level" (Rankine, "Interview by Lauren Berlant"). Dehumanizing a Black person and displacing her from her own body, consciously or unconsciously, makes it easier for white people to perpetuate the aggressions recorded in *Citizen*.

With her acute attention to writing the body, Rankine presents a searing description of how the wounds of racism can feel: "Certain moments send adrenaline to the heart, dry out the tongue, and clog the lungs. Like thunder they drown you in sound, no, like lightning they strike you across the larynx. Cough. After it happened I was at a loss for words" (7). Showing what the experiences of daily racism feel like physically, Rankine humanizes the Black subjects she writes about. Poet and critic Elisabeth Frost argues that the focus on embodied experience is fundamental to Rankine's project. "Rankine's work strives toward an elusive but crucial goal: to replace spectacle with sensation and affect, with lived, embodied experience. In *Citizen*, the danger and vulnerability of that embodiment come into dramatic relief" (Frost 169). *Citizen* puts readers inside the scope of experience rather than allowing them to remain outside, as removed spectators.

Furthermore, throughout Rankine's work, she explores what it means to inhabit silence because of trauma, to be silenced by another person, and to be "at a loss for words." The inhabitation of this silence can be the grounds for Black citizenship: "Yes, and this is how you are a citizen: Come on. Let it go. Move on" (151). The Black citizen is forced into a condition of silence and acceptance. For example, in the script for the video poem "Stop-and-Frisk," Rankine writes:

All living is listening for a throat to open—
The length of its silence shaping lives.

When he opened his mouth to speak, his speech
was what was written in the silence,

The length of the silence becoming a living. (112)

This selection shows that to be alive, to be fully human, is to listen to others: "All living is listening for a throat to open" else silence itself becomes what we live, with unacknowledged racism that irrevocably wounds the individual and social body.

The poem script for "Stop-and-Frisk" begins with the following situation:

I knew whatever was in front of me was happening and then the police vehicle came to a screeching halt in front of me like they were setting up a blockade. Everywhere were flashes, a siren sounding and a stretched-out roar. Get on the ground. Get on the ground now. Then I just knew (105).

Several phrases are repeated throughout the script, including "stretched-out roar" (105, 106, 107) and "Get on the ground" (105, 106), showing how repetitive the "Stop-and-Frisk" situation has become for those disproportionately affected by such policies. For example, "In 1999, Blacks and Latinos made up 50 percent of New York's population, but accounted for 84 percent" of New Yorkers who were stopped by police (Thompson).

In the video poem, a pair of young Black men enter a sneaker and clothing boutique. Two other young Black men are already shopping in the store. They all enjoy trying on hoodies and jackets and pulling some sneaker styles off the shelf to show one another, before one makes a purchase and he and his friend leave the store. The men remaining in the store are smiling and interacting with one another on this casual shopping expedition. We never hear them speak. This scene would remain pleasant, though unremarkable, if not for the soundtrack and the images projected on the men in the video poem. The viewer sees a number of lights flashing simultaneously: a flashing blue and white police siren, as well as flashing yellow lights. The lights are visible through their reflection in the glass window of the store, as if a police car with flashing lights is pointed toward the storefront (Lucas, "Claudia Rankine's Poem 'Stop and Frisk'"). The effect is disturbing and obscures the entire frame of the young men enjoying one another's company. The lights demonstrate that young Black men are under surveillance even as they are going about their daily lives, doing ordinary things. Though it is impossible to know this from just watching the video, the actors in the video poem are students at Pomona College, where Rankine was a professor at the time.

The soundtrack to the video poem is layered with: ominous musical chords played on an organ, several screeching police sirens, Rankine (offscreen) reading her video poem script, an undercurrent of police radio chat, and the voice of President Barack Obama making a statement. All of this is played simultaneously, as is the video of the young men shopping and the video of lights flashing, over which these soundtracks are heard. Though the shopping scene at first appears pleasant, the additions to the video suggest impending danger. In one of the looping soundtracks two voices repeat: "You don't know why? I don't know why." The video poem ends with these words (Lucas, "Claudia Rankine's Poem 'Stop and Frisk'"). These questions echo those from the poem script: "Then why are you pulling me over? Why am I pulled over?" (106).

Returning to the poem's title, which provides the framing for the video poem, Cornell Law School's Legal Information Institute explains the term, "stop-and-frisk," which Rankine also uses as the title poem:

A stop-and-frisk refers to a brief non-intrusive police stop of a suspect. The Fourth Amendment requires that before stopping the suspect, the police must have a reasonable suspicion that a crime has been, is being, or is about to be committed by the suspect. If the police reasonably suspect that the suspect is armed and dangerous, the police may frisk the suspect, meaning that the police will give a quick pat-down of the suspect's outer clothing. ("Stop and Frisk").

Despite the suggestion that this type of stop would include a "quick pat-down," the NYPD's policy was disproportionately and violently applied to Black and Latinx New Yorkers; thus, another phrase is repeated in the poem script: "And you were not the guy yet still you fit the description because there is only one guy who is always the guy fitting the description" (108, 109), showing that African Americans and Latinos as a group, as well as individual Black and Latinx men, are repeatedly assumed to be "the guy fitting the description."

Neither "reasonable" nor "quick," the officers in the poem script physically abuse the men they profile, in a scene similar to those captured by citizen's cell phone videos, cop or "sky" cams, and sometimes police body cams or dash cams throughout the U.S.: "you are stretched on the hood" (106). Or, a man reports, "I was pulled out of my vehicle a block from my door, handcuffed and pushed into the vehicle's backseat, the officer's knee pressing into my collarbone" (107). Yet an almost more important aim appears to be the officers' intent to humiliate: "Yes officer rolled around on my tongue, which grew out of a bell that could never ring because its emergency was a tolling I was meant to swallow" (105); "the officer's warm breath vacating a face creased into a smile of its own private joke" (107); "I was told, after the fingerprinting, to stand naked" (109).

And whether the men speak or are silent, comply quickly or not quickly enough, are innocent or guilty, the results are the same: "Each time it begins in the same way, it doesn't begin the same way, each time it begins it's the same" (107). In the video poem, some lines from the printed script are revised and expanded. For example, "I was told, after the fingerprinting to stand naked. I stood naked. It was only then that I was instructed to dress, to leave, to walk all those miles home" (109) becomes, in the video poem: "After the fingerprinting, I was told to strip, presumably to allow his charge to be put on display. I stood there naked before being instructed to dress, to leave, to walk all those miles home" (Lucas, "Claudia Rankine's Poem 'Stop and Frisk'"). The addition of "presumably to allow his charge to be put on display" emphasizes the officer's intent to humiliate the man he has arrested.

The repetition of the police officers' actions wears down a population of people of color who are not guilty of any crime: "In a landscape drawn from an ocean bed, you can't drive yourself sane—so angry you are crying. You can't drive yourself sane. This motion wears a guy out. Our motion is wearing you out and still you are not that guy" (105). These situations may drive the men to insanity, as thoughts and statements accumulate. "You can't drive yourself sane. You are not insane. Our motion is wearing you out. You are not the guy" (107). Even if "you are not the guy," you will be worn down by these abuses. Even though you assure yourself that "you are not insane," you cannot drive yourself back to sanity.

Rankine demonstrates in *Citizen* that these experiences of daily aggression and structural racism are not fleeting experiences but are "stored" in the body: "The world is wrong. You can't put the past behind you. It's buried in you; it's turned your flesh into its own cupboard. Not everything remembered is useful but it all comes from the world to be stored in you" (Rankine 63). The "storing" of trauma in the physical body is not only metaphor. Bessel van der Kolk's work as a researcher and therapist demonstrates that trauma actually "interferes with the brain circuits" and can "literally reshape both brain and body" (van der Kolk). Traumatized people may have difficulty with focusing, memory, overwhelming emotions such as "incomprehensible anxiety," and other stressors that interfere with everyday life. Other scientific research also shows that trauma alters the body.

For example, "epigenetics," an emerging field of scientific research, "shows how environmental influences— children's experiences—actually affect the expression of their genes" (*What Is Epigenetics?*). This research further shows that "the epigenome can be affected by positive experiences, …or negative influences, such as environmental toxins or stressful life circumstances, which leave a unique epigenetic 'signature' on the genes'" (*What Is Epigenetics?*). Thus, "[w]hen experiences during development rearrange the epigenetic marks that govern gene expression, they can change whether and how genes release the information they carry" (*What Is Epigenetics?*). Previously it was believed that the genes children inherit from their parents govern their development, but experiences—both positive and negative—can also affect how those genes are expressed.

Indeed, some geneticists argue, "[i]Inheritance of genomic DNA underlies the vast majority of biological inheritance, yet it has been clear for decades that additional epigenetic information can be passed on to future generations" (Bošković and Rando). This process has been described in several ways, including "transgenerational epigenetic inheritance," "epigenetic inheritance," or "intergenerational trauma" that can be passed on through at least a few generations. "Epigenetic inheritance is an unconventional finding. It goes against the idea that inheritance happens only through the DNA code that passes from parent to offspring. It means that a parent's *experiences*, in the form of epigenetic tags, can be passed down

133

to future generations" (emphasis added) ("Epigenetics & Inheritance"). These embodied experiences remained stored in the flesh's "cupboard" whether they are spoken of or not, but the work of *Citizen* demonstrates the roles that speaking, writing, and making art can play in moving these traumas into a place not only of individual, but also societal, resolution in order to ameliorate what Frost calls the "effects of our culture's denials about race on both individual and social bodies" (186). Wounds that are not brought to the surface and resolved remain to be passed on to others.

Addressing the traumas and historic erasure of Black men, Glenn Ligon's *Untitled (Speech/Crowd) #2* is included within the "Stop-and-Frisk" poem script (108-109). *Untitled (Speech/Crowd) #2* began with a photo of men at the 1995 Million Man March in Washington, D.C., that Ligon enlarged over and over until the men's faces were obscured. The media used in this piece include "silkscreen, coal dust, oilstick, ink, glue on paper," creating a gritty, almost illegible image that employs varying shades of black (*Citizen* 165). This piece is part of a series. Another work in the series, *Untitled (Speech/Crowd) #3*, uses text from a speech given at the Million Man March layered with a black-and-white photograph of the attendees.

> Visibility and legibility are often themes explored in Ligon's text-based works through the interplay of text and choice of background. Here, text and image make each other difficult to read, and the work focuses instead on varied densities of Black tone that suggest the march's mission of gathering diverse Black perspectives.
> (Ligon, *Untitled (Speech/Crowd) #3*)

The visibility of Black men as individuals and the assertion of agency of Black men as a group are some of important themes of Ligon's series.

Planned by Louis Farrakhan, the leader of the Nation of Islam, and former NAACP Executive Secretary Benjamin Chavis, the Million Man March began as a response to issues exposed during the LA riots and a desire to focus on issues affecting Black men. The U.S. Park Police wildly underestimated "that 400,000 people had attended, angering the Million Man March's organizers. A later estimate put the number at 870,000 with a 20 percent margin of error," (History.com Editors) underscoring Ligon's theme of Black erasure. According to the Amistad Digital Resource at Columbia University, however, the march "was without question the largest single gathering of black people in U.S. history," drawing close to a million people ("The Million Man March"). The march also contributed to lasting social and political changes: "Within the next year, over 1.5 million black men registered to vote" ("The Million Man March").

The first two of Ligon's *Untitled: Four Etchings* (1992) are reproduced on pages 52 and 53. This series also engages the theme of Black visibility and erasure. The panels as a group use quotes from Zora Neale Hurston's essay, "How It Feels to Be Colored Me" (1928), and Ralph Ellison's novel *Invisible Man* (1952). In the first etching, the phrase "I DO NOT ALWAYS FEEL COLORED" is repeated (52) and in the second, the phrase "I FEEL MOST COLORED WHEN I AM THROWN AGAINST A SHARP WHITE BACKGROUND" is used, both of which are drawn from Hurston's essay (53). It is possible to read the text on the first two etchings, though the words become more blurred toward the bottom of the page. In the third of the series, a shadow of words is suggested, but the text cannot be read, and in the fourth, the page appears almost entirely black (Ligon, *Untitled: Four Etchings*. 1992, *The Metropolitan Museum of Art*). The last two prints are "printed in black on black to render them intentionally hard to decipher, [and] repeat the first lines of Ralph Ellison's 1952 novel *Invisible Man* (Ligon, *Untitled (Four*

Etchings). 1992, *Cleveland Museum of Art*). Not only does this series emphasize visibility and invisibility, it also highlights the connections between seeing and reading. "Ligon's manipulations of the text navigate the differences between seeing and reading, and the reliability of the ways in which people see and read each other" ("Glenn Ligon - Bio | The Broad"). Ligon enacts these themes through physical manipulations of the text.

This effect is enabled by the medium he chooses: "Taking advantage of the textures achievable with etching and aquatint techniques, Ligon here creates two black-on-white and two black-on-black prints whose dense layers and deliberate smudges visualize themes of legibility and illegibility, prominence and erasure, and blackness and whiteness" (Ligon, *Untitled: Four Etchings*. 1992, *The Metropolitan Museum of Art*). The medium is described in *Citizen* as "soft ground etchings, aquatint, spitbite, and sugarlift aquatint in black on Rives BKF paper" (164). Aquatint is "a printmaking technique that produces tonal effects by using acid to eat into the printing plate creating sunken areas which hold the ink" ("Aquatint"). The form itself enacts erasure through its use of acid. Moreover, the pooling of ink in the print plate creates splotches hampering legibility. A sugar lift, a form of aquatint etching, "is a way of creating painterly marks on an etching plate using a sugar solution and a paint brush" ("Sugar Lift Etching"). Picasso used the sugar lift method for some of his most notable etchings. Ligon uses this historical technique to simultaneously present beauty and struggle.

The themes in "Stop-and-Frisk" and in Ligon's artwork represent traumatic experience that African Americans regularly endure in everyday life. It can be rare for Black people to share these lived experiences and vulnerabilities with a white audience; keeping these experiences within the Black community can be a form of self-preservation. Thus, in "We Wear the Mask," a rondeau first collected in the 1895 book of poems *Majors and Minors*, Paul Laurence Dunbar writes: "We wear the mask that

136

grins and lies, / It hides our cheeks and shades our eyes,—"
(Dunbar, "We Wear the Mask"). Why risk exposing oneself to
people who can, and often do, cause further harm?

> Why should the world be over-wise,
> In counting all our tears and sighs?
> Nay, let them only see us, while
>> We wear the mask. (Dunbar, "We Wear the Mask")

Scholar James Smethurst explains how "Dunbar's notion of the
masking of one's true nature..." is linked to "a more strictly
legalistic sense of post-Reconstruction Jim Crow segregation"
and the central "problem of being a citizen and yet not a citizen
(and, by extension, of being legally human and not quite human
at the same time)" (378), a central subject around which *Citizen*
revolves. Masking is necessary for protection when segregation
and discrimination are enshrined in laws, and violent methods of
their enforcement are common.

Reading Rankine's exploration of the concept of
citizenship, which she emphasizes in the title, requires an
understanding of the ways in which African Americans have not
enjoyed full citizenship rights before Dunbar and after, into the
present day. "As Rankine shows, the notion of citizenship itself
takes on different meanings for people of various subject
positions, depending on one's always already racialized position
in relation to it. For this reason, even ostensibly definitive
qualifiers like 'lyric' or 'American' operate, and demand to be
read, ironically," writes poet and literary critic Angela Hume
(Hume 104-105). Thus, although the twenty-first century may
appear different than the Jim Crow era, readers must consider
that the experiences recalled in *Citizen* exist on a historical
continuum, to understand where we are now as a nation: "This
complicated there/here dynamic provides an historical
understanding of racism's permanence," writes scholar Bella

Adams (Adams 59). Rankine, Beth Loffreda, and Max Cap King articulate this "there/here dynamic"—what I am calling the historical continuum—in their introduction to *The Racial Imaginary: Writers on Race in the Life of the Mind*: "We're still there—there differently than those before us, but there, otherwise known as here" (Rankine et al. 13). The social body is made up of generations of people and texts connected across time, both there (the past) and here (the present) connected along the historical continuum.

Collecting other people's stories and combining them with her own through the second person "you" also enables a unique crossing of genres. Bringing these stories together not only advances Rankine's continuing project of focusing on the social, but also produces in the reader a better understanding of race and power. Significantly, this method also results in a book that has the unique distinction of being a best-seller in both the poetry and non-fiction categories. In a conversation with Berlant, Rankine remarks,

> The entire book is a collection of stories gathered from a community of friends and then retold or folded into my own stories. And though it's not strictly nonfiction, *Citizen* is not fiction either. The experience of writing it, which might or might not be the experience of reading it, was to see my community a little better, to see it, to understand my place in it, to know how it sounds, what it looks like, and yet, to stay on my street anyway. (Rankine, "Interview by Lauren Berlant")

A traditional understanding of lyric poetry, linked by some scholars to the Romantic era, maintains that the lyric "I" reveals subjective, private feeling; whereas non-fiction, of course, dwells in the realm of purported facts. *Citizen*'s dual genre status (that is, the way it is received by readers as both poetry and non-fiction)

138

thus requires a seemingly incongruous crossing of the categories of personal feeling and objective facts. Yet, like her previous books, Rankine is troubling generic categories. With a focus on storytelling, *Citizen* employs narrative as its primary device, within the larger form of social documentary.

However, some scholars still make sense of this incongruity by considering how *Citizen* modifies the lyric. For example, Mary-Jean Chan argues that in modifying the conventional lyric "I," with her use of the second person "you," in what Chan labels "lyric hybridity," Rankine is able further to demonstrate power inequalities: "Whilst conventional uses of the lyric tend to feature a singular poetic voice at work, Rankine chooses to emphasize the relationality of the lyric 'I' vis-à-vis the second or third person in order to accentuate the unequal power relations that exist between racialized bodies" (Chan 140). Social documentary can accommodate lyric beside other genres, but *Citizen* tell stories in a way not applicable to conventional modes of lyric. To address someone as "you" can deny them their individuality, which is an important point of emphasis in the work.

Indeed, being addressed, "hey, you!" rather than by one's name can be dehumanizing. Thus, "Rankine hints at the power that the white 'I' has over the diminished 'you'—since to refer to another person simply as 'you' is a demeaning form of address: a way of emotionally displacing someone from the security of their own body" (Chan 140). More, *Citizen* demonstrates that this calling out of "you" can cause Black people to be "hypervisible in the face of such language acts" (49). Thus, *Citizen* demonstrates the harm created not only when Black people are ignored and rendered invisible, but also when those actions create "hypervisibility." In Section III, the speaker reports:

For so long you thought the ambition of racist language was to denigrate and erase you as a person. After considering

Butler's remarks, you begin to understand yourself as
rendered hypervisible in the face of such language acts.
Language that feels hurtful is intended to exploit all the ways
that you are present. Your alertness, your openness, your
looking up, your talking back, and as insane as it is, saying
please. (49)

Here, "you" are attending a talk given by theorist Judith Butler
that highlights how racist language aggressively renders the
Black person "hypervisible," all eyes turned upon them, when
any response, from being open to "talking back," exploits "your"
presence and is perceived as wrong, even shameful. "[S]aying
please" shows the need all people have to be understood: please
understand, please recognize me as human, which is labeled
"insane" because such a basic need is denied when the humanity
of Black people is denied. Continuing to demand this recognition
in situations that repeatedly deny it can feel insane. This and
other passages exhort readers to consider what the "sane"
response in such situations might be. How do Black citizens keep
themselves sane in the face of repeated injuries that deny their
personhood?

Alternatively, the book also explores what it may mean
for a Black subject to inhabit the "I," to be subject rather than
object.

Sometimes "I" is supposed to hold what is not there until it is.
Then *what is* comes apart the closer you are to it.

This makes the first person a symbol for something.

The pronoun barely holding the person together. (71)

The lyric "I" is supposed to "hold what is not there until it is"
making it a symbol for a whole subject/person, but here the

pronoun can barely hold the person together. Discussing who has the power to inhabit the "I" and her choice to use the second person point of view in *Citizen*, Rankine notes, "I also wanted to put a little bit of pressure on the sense of who has power, who can stand in that 'I' versus who can't, and, talking specifically about African-Americans, on the notion that we started as property. The notion that personhood came *after* objecthood, that the move into the 'I' was actually—insanely—a step that had to be taken legally" (Rankine, "On Being Seen: An Interview with Claudia Rankine from Ferguson"). This particularly American insanity can be traced through the successive and continuous legal attempts to grant African Americans the status of personhood and the rights of citizenship, such as the Thirteenth, Fourteenth, and Fifteenth Amendments to the *Constitution*.

Moreover, Skillman argues that the "complicity of Enlightenment humanism in defining white humanity against black subhumanity, in enshrining white freedom through black enslavement, deeply complicates the trope of lyric presence in the context of African American literary aesthetics" (Skillman 436). However, Rankine's "I" in this section holds a space, fighting for Black subjectivity, while also demonstrating the contradictions a Black poet may encounter in the use of the lyric poetic form that presupposes a universal, transcendent subject that does not include them.

Showing that the experiences of erasure and hypervisibility begin in childhood, Section I of *Citizen* begins with an interaction between two twelve-year-old girls in Catholic school. The speaker explains: "the girl sitting behind you asks you to lean to the right during exams so she can copy what you have written" (5). Later down the page, the reader learns more about the two girls' interactions: "You never really speak except for the time she makes her request and later when she tells you you smell good and have features more like a white person. You assume she thinks she is thanking you for letting her cheat and feels better cheating from an almost white person" (5). This opening allows the reader to understand how the reverberations of racially-marked interactions are carried from childhood into adulthood. The child whose paper is being copied both understands and feels the painful, racist assumptions embedded in being thought of as "almost white." Moreover, the Black girl is invisible to the white girl as an individual: they never really speak, the white girl exploits the Black girl's intelligence, and can only apply white standards of beauty to judge her in a supposed complement that simultaneously denigrates the Black child. This might seem to be a small interaction, something the young girl should just "get over," but by spotlighting the child's experience, Rankine demands that readers understand its importance and how it interrupts larger national narratives about the experiences of democracy and freedom.

In retelling the stories of these encounters, Rankine also hopes to show how personal experiences of racism and structural racism are connected. She explains, "On the one hand, I am talking about institutionalized racism. But on another and, I think, equally important level, I'm just talking about what happens when we fail each other as people" (Westervelt). Importantly, as Hume argues, this failure is also a failure of language, a theme that *Citizen* emphasizes: "In the failure of the most basic attempts to communicate in language, the structural edicts of racism that even language must struggle against come sharply into relief" (Hume 104). Rankine's recording of such a wide variety of what we might call these failed encounters and the failure of language thus builds upon itself, creating a layered and intense reading experience.

As Cocozza notes, "Soon, these small, private experiences—which Rankine gathered from her own life and from friends' anecdotes—begin to accumulate." Each vignette exposes a picture from the larger life of race and racism in America to also illustrate how these private experiences are related to larger, global events so that "[s]oon this private world of solitarily experienced, silently swallowed incidents erupts into the sphere of public event and global notice" (Cocozza). These spheres include police shootings of unarmed African Americans, as well as the federal government's failure to protect Black citizens in other contexts.

In fact, Rankine first began writing what became *Citizen* in response to a large national tragedy: the governmental inaction both before and after Hurricane Katrina (which made landfall off the coast of Louisiana on August 29, 2005) that led to chaos and destruction of human life. In a 2016 interview published in the *Paris Review*, she relates the following:

> I worked on *Citizen* on and off for almost ten years. I wrote the first piece in response to Hurricane Katrina. I was profoundly moved by the events in New Orleans as they unfolded. John and I taped the CNN coverage of the storm without any real sense of what we intended to do with the material. I didn't think, obviously, that I was working on *Citizen*. But for me, there is no push and pull. There's no private world that doesn't include the dynamics of my political and social world. (Rankine, "Interview by David L. Ulin")

Rankine's merging of the private with the political emerges from a history of feminist writing and activism. For example, according to poet and activist Audre Lorde (1934-1992), in her well-known essay "The Master's Tools Will Never Dismantle the Master's House," in order to address racism, sexism, and homophobia each woman must "...reach down into that deep place of knowledge inside herself and touch that terror and loathing of any difference that lives there. See whose face it wears. Then the personal as the political can begin to illuminate all our choices" (Lorde, "The Master's Tools" 111). Lorde views differences (in race, class, gender, sexuality) as energy rather than (only) injury. Thus becoming educated about and valuing these differences in oneself and others—rather than denying, fearing, or "loathing" them—women as a collective can create positive social change, rather than remaining divided.

This is similar to Rankine's call in *Citizen* for readers to recognize how their own personal roles and choices, as reflected in the encounters being described, might reinforce or potentially dismantle racism. In conversation with Rankine, Berlant draws attention to "how writing can allow us to amplify overwhelming scenes of ordinary violence while interrupting the sense of a fated stuckness" (Rankine, "Interview by Lauren Berlant"). Thus, when the encounters reveal how "race happens," in the everyday, readers can consider ways that they may redo or revise these power dynamics interpersonally and socially.

One of the first articulations of "the personal is political" can be traced to Carol Hanisch's essay published in *Notes from the Second Year: Women's Liberation* in 1970. She explains that it was the editors, Shulamith Firestone and Anne Koedt, who decided to call her essay, "The Personal Is Political." Hanisch notes: "One of the first things we discovered in these [Women's Liberation Movement consciousness raising] groups is that personal problems are political problems" (Hanisch). This discovery was particularly important in revealing how power relations in male/female, white/black, owner/worker and other relationships emanate from structural inequalities and are not the "fault" of the person being oppressed. Thus, the pain and anger the Black woman feels when her white friend unthinkingly addresses her by her Black housekeeper's name is not a simple "personal problem," but rather a symptom of racial inequalities and the ways in which people fail to recognize others across racial lines. Or, when victims of Hurricane Katrina were unable to get out of the storm's path, their so-called "failure" to evacuate must be understood in relation to two centuries of structural inequalities.

Thus, Hurricane Katrina, as the impetus for the writing of *Citizen*, is an important event for readers to remember and analyze in order to understand how the delayed emergency response was related to the perceived social status of the storm's victims. Yet, Michael Brown, FEMA director under then-president George W. Bush, blamed the citizens' "failure to evacuate" instead of taking responsibility for FEMA's inaction. "Another line of attack, playing on the stereotype of the shiftless South, was to imply that the citizenry had been too indolent to get out of harm's way," *Washington Post* reporter Jed Horne writes. Horne quotes Brown, who told Congress a month after Katrina, "The failure to evacuate was the tipping point for all the other things that either went wrong or were exacerbated." But thousands of people in New Orleans were trapped, without access to transportation that could take them to safety, which the emergency response team seemingly failed to grasp, or used as an excuse to blame the victims of the hurricane. "Tens of thousands of New Orleanians were trapped in the Superdome and the city's Convention Center," Horne notes, "The Louisiana National Guard had asked FEMA for 700 buses; days later, the agency sent 100, and nearly a week had passed before the last flood survivors were herded aboard" (Horne). The waiting for aid extended beyond what anyone in New Orleans could imagine in the face of such an extreme emergency.

Thus, Rankine's and Lucas's video poem names other deadly forces, in addition to drowning, among them dehydration, overheating, and "no electricity, no power, no way to communicate" (Lucas, "August 29, 2005/Hurricane Katrina")— that survivors of the initial flooding faced. The flooding had progressed rapidly; within an hour of the National Weather Service issuing a flood warning, "the neighborhood known as the Lower Ninth Ward was under six-to-eight feet of water. . . . By the next day, eighty percent of New Orleans lay underwater, in some areas to a height of twenty feet" ("Today in History - August 29 - Hurricane Katrina"). The wait for rescue, day after day, stole the lives of people who could have been saved. Rankine explains that "[t]he scripts in chapter six seemed necessary to *Citizen* because one of the questions I often hear is 'How did that happen?' as it relates to mind-numbing moments of injustice—the aftermath of Katrina, for example, or juries letting supremacists off with a slap on the wrist for killing black men" (Berlant, "Claudia Rankine by Lauren Berlant").

Rankine thus seeks to inform readers how seemingly small interactions between people of different races, such as a white man cutting in front of a Black woman in line because she is invisible to him—"Oh my God, I didn't see you. / You must be in a hurry, you offer. / No, no, no. I really didn't see you." (77)— are connected to large tragedies, including police killings of unarmed African Americans. Williams powerfully expresses the violent effects of white's inability to see Black people:

> . . . white people see all the worlds beyond me but not me.
> They come trotting at me with force and speed; they do not
> see me. I could force my presence, the real me contained in
> those eyes, upon them, but I would be smashed in the process.
> If I deflect, if I move out of the way, they will never know I
> existed. (12)

Thus, these daily interactions, Rankine asserts, are potent indicators of the resultant structural racism: "It seems obvious, but I don't think we connect micro-aggressions that indicate the lack of recognition of the black body as a body to the creation and enforcement of laws. Everyone is cool with seeing micro-aggressions as misunderstandings until the same misunderstood person ends up on a jury or running national response teams after a hurricane" (Rankine, "Interview by Lauren Berlant").

Rankine's poem script, "August 29, 2005 / Hurricane Katrina," thus links the injury forged by daily racism (not recognizing the Black body as a human body) with large scale injury and death brought about by structural racism.

For Hume, "Rankine's *Citizen* registers and ironizes the continued intertwining of state violence, racism, and the environment when she quotes the words of one Katrina survivor: 'I don't know what the water wanted. It wanted to show you no one would come' (85). Yet, "[e]ven before Katrina," Hume argues,

> black communities in New Orleans were subject to a greater degree of environmental risk. . . . Rankine's poem points toward society's collective denial of what the facts themselves would seem to lay bare: that an entire population was not perceived as valuable enough to warrant taking preventive measures to ensure its safety in general, including its safety in the case of a major storm along the Gulf Coast. (83)

Hume's point of view is shared by others who were on the ground in New Orleans during the storm. For example, Douglas Brinkley, Katrina survivor and author of *The Great Deluge,* an account of the flooding in New Orleans (who also appears in Spike Lee's award-winning documentary, *When the Levees Broke: A Requiem in Four Acts*), strongly argues that governmental inaction created the human disaster: "What became apparent to Spike and me as we collaborated was that Katrina, in New Orleans anyway, was a man-made disaster. At least 700 fellow citizens wouldn't have died if the levee system and pumping stations had done their jobs properly" (Brinkley). Others estimate that the death toll as a direct result of the storm was as high as 1,200 (Gibbens).

Indeed, despite initial claims by federal officials to the contrary, it became apparent that "key levees, including the 17th

Street and London Avenue canals in the heart of the city, failed with water well below levels they were designed to withstand" (Horne). Horne further explains:

> As the Army Corps eventually conceded, they [the levees] were breached because of flawed engineering and collapsed because they were junk. Sheet piling—metal planks driven into the ground to reinforce levees and flood walls—didn't run deep enough. Corps geologists botched tests that should have determined soil stability below the levees. The Corps and local levee boards that maintain flood barriers pinched pennies, and suddenly Katrina became the nation's first $200 billion disaster. (Horne)

As Lucas and Rankine stress, however, the greatest cost was the suffering and death of many of New Orleans's poorest residents.

Highlighting this human cost, the black-and-white images taken during the storm that are used in the video poem focus on people, primarily African Americans. Numerous people are wading through the flood waters as best as they can, sometimes in water that is chest high. Others use ladders to climb up onto roofs to wait for rescue, while others make their way in small, private boats. Still others have drowned—we see the excruciating images of their bodies floating, face down in the water. The only color in the video poem is the swirling image of the hurricane, dominated by a sickly fluorescent green, which obscures the view of the people, and the only sound—other than Rankine reading the poem script—is of frighteningly high winds and rain (Lucas, "August 29, 2005/Hurricane Katrina"). The video poem prompts the viewer to be with the people in the storm, while also suggesting that the mainstream repetition of these images results in a majority population that is inured to black suffering and death, particularly when it is played over and over on television.

Like Rankine, Spike Lee was watching the news coverage of Katrina on television. In Italy for the Venice Film Festival, Lee notes that he was "… just holed up in my hotel room switching back and forth between the BBC and CNN. And every day I wondered when is the federal government going to show up" (Gordon). "And very early on, I recognized I was watching a historic moment in American history," Lee reports (Gordon). Interviewer Ed Gordon relates his experience of watching Lee's *When the Levees Broke:* "When you watch this, it really is just a grouping of stories. And when you meet the people and hear the stories, it really does tell this story in a different way than just watching the news accounts." Strikingly, this form of retelling is in concert with how Rankine chose to structure *Citizen.* "I didn't have to make the thing up," says Lee, "The federal government took five days to show up. President Bush took 12 days to show up." (Gordon).

The exhaustive experience of waiting is present in both *Citizen* and *When the Levees Broke.* The speaker in *Citizen* explains what it was like to be inside the storm, waiting for rescue.

> Hours later, still in the difficulty of what it is to be, just like that, inside it, standing there, maybe wading, maybe waving, standing where the deep waters of everything backed up, one said, climbing over bodies, one said, stranded on a roof, one said, trapped in the building, and in the difficulty, nobody coming and still someone saying, who could see it coming, the difficulty of that. (Rankine 83)

Within the poem's description of the storm, Rankine records both the observations of CNN commentators, whom she was watching on television as the storm unfolded, as well as the voices of storm survivors who were interviewed ("one said"). Hume notes that the poem's "…repetition of the attributive phrase 'one said,' …

emphasizes the fact of so many individual experiences of being forced to wait for aid" (83). Collectively, these individuals' experiences form a weight upon the reader of the poem scripts in the book, making reading an exhausting experience. Rankine achieves this through repetition and the grammatical construction of long individual sentences.

> The repetition of the phrase within a single long sentence demands endurance of the reader, too—of both the upsetting imagery and the exhausting sentence. Reading becomes duration, and this duration becomes exasperating when the sentence culminates with "who could see it coming," a clause that is deflated and made all the more "difficult" in being denied its question mark (Hume 83).

Indeed, it is evident that there were those who *could* see it coming, yet failed to provide protection to New Orleans's most vulnerable people anyway, and then also failed to provide aid once the storm hit. "Who could see it coming" is presented as a statement, rather than a question, because the speaker already knows that officials were in possession of information concerning the storm's magnitude and how it would progress.

The "slow waiting" and suffering of the citizens waiting for aid in New Orleans recalls Berlant's assertion that such a precarious state of living is "life-in-death" or "slow death." Berlant describes this experience as "the physical wearing out of a population in a way that points to its deterioration as a defining condition of its experience and historical existence" (Berlant 95) while Hume, who focuses on Rankine's "engagement with embodied experiences of racism and environmental risk," (80) reads "*Citizen* as the latest installment of Rankine's twenty-year meditation on the 'wasting body' [showing how] certain bodies are attenuated or made sick under capitalism and the state, while simultaneously being regarded as surplus" (Hume 79). Surplus, that state of being "left over" or "extra," is embodied in the poem script in the descriptions of human bodies left behind in the storm amongst the rubble:

> Then each house was a mumbling structure, all that water, buildings peeling apart, the yellow foam, the contaminated drawl of mildew, mold.
>
> The missing limb, he said, the bodies lodged in piles of rubble, dangling from rafters, lying facedown, arms outstretched on parlor floors.
>
> And someone said, where were the buses? And simultaneously someone else said, FEMA said it wasn't safe to be there. (84)

As Hume contends, "the detritus left in the wake of the storm" contains not only "ruined homes and objects, but also human detritus, bodies in pieces" (Hume 83). Rankine blurs the lines between human and object, demonstrating how human beings left behind in the rubble are regarded as objects to be discarded. The "missing limb" may first appear to be that of a tree, yet here trees, human bodies, and rubble merge. Moreover, objects are anthropomorphized—the houses are "mumbling" as the mildew emits a "contaminated drawl"—while the people abandoned in the storm have no voice. Finally, another irony emerges as someone recalls that "FEMA said it wasn't safe to be there," while the people inside the storm continue to wait (84).

Lee also highlights experiences of waiting in his film. Recalling an interview with Junior Rodriguez, president of St. Bernard's Parish in the City of New Orleans, Lee explains that Rodriquez, "talked about how he would sit in this office trying to keep things together," waiting for the federal government to take action, when, quite unexpectedly, "in walked into his office a commander from the Royal Canadian Mounties. He said, where are you from? He said, we're from Canada? Where in Canada? They were from Vancouver" (Gordon). Vancouver, a Western seaport city in British Columbia, is 2,725 miles from New Orleans. Lee extrapolates on what seems to be an almost unreal contrast, "How is it Dudley Do Right guys—I used to watch that cartoon growing up—how it is a company of Dudley Do Rights can make it to New Orleans from Vancouver, and they had horses too, how can they make it to New Orleans before the federal government? That's crazy" (Gordon). While the two projects, Lee's documentary and the video poems, bear similarities, Rankine's and Lucas's video poem genre differs from the documentary genre in their aim to create a state of "indwelling" or being inside of the scene (inside the storm) rather than being outside, a removed spectator.

"Situation 5," (the script titled "February 26, 2012 / In Memory of Trayvon Martin in *Citizen*) also explores the tension between "looking at" vs. "being with." The primary video image is of different Black men riding alone in vehicles quietly gazing out sometimes rainy windows, what Rankine has called "being in their dailiness." The video poem's voiceover, which differs slightly from the text in *Citizen* (89-90), begins, "My brothers are notorious. Even though they have never been to prison, they are imprisoned" and goes on to note that "the hearts of my brothers are broken" (Rankine and Lucas, "Situation 5"). Toward the middle of the 4 minute, 32 second video poem, a quick series of still images from Jim Crow America appear on the right side of the screen, including a picture of Emmett Till, a prison work gang, a "help wanted" sign that states "whites only," segregated busses, and a noose hanging from a tree. Thereafter, additional video is layered onto the still-present video of the men riding alone in cars, including footage of LAPD officers beating Black motorist Rodney King as he lay on the ground.

Near the end of the video, a quote from poet Lyn Hejinian appears on the screen, giving us insight into the title of the video series: "Nothing is isolated in history— / certain humans are situations" (Rankine and Lucas, "Situation 5"). By insisting that the viewer look deeply into the situations of everyday life, the videos prompt the observer to consider their own place in the social order and the history embedded in those encounters. "There are two worlds out there; two America's out there," Rankine asserts:

> If you're a white person, there's one way of being a citizen in our country; and if you're a brown or a black body, there's another way of being a citizen and that way is very close to death. It's very close to the loss of your life. It's very close to the loss of your liberties at any random moment. And so I wanted that to be considered (Westervelt)

These facts are highlighted with the insertion of a historical photograph at the end of the poem script written for Trayvon Martin, underscoring the ongoing precarity of African American life across the historical continuum (91).

Appearing in Section VI with the poem script, "February 26, 2012 / In Memory of Trayvon Martin," the photograph, titled "Public Lynching," and dated August 30, 1930, is a "well-known photograph of a lynching, from which Ms. Rankine has removed the hanging Black bodies, highlighting the excited faces of the white mob,"(Lee) suggesting that Martin's murder was a vigilante lynching. Considering lynching historically as "ritualized murder," Koritha Mitchell argues that the "predictable steps, and their standardization across the country, reflected white agreement with mainstream declarations that African Americans were immoral and bestial, that they were not citizens and perhaps not fully human" (Mitchell 24). Mitchell shows, therefore, that "when lynching became racially motivated, it also became theatrical ..." (24). Rather than being drawn into the "theatre" of ritualized murder and the spectacle of dead Black bodies,

Rankine stresses the need to "redirect our gaze" to the white spectators (Lee).

Historian Amy Louise Wood notes that lynch mobs enacted images of white power and invented Black criminality "that served to instill and perpetuate a sense of racial supremacy in their white spectators" (Wood 2). This was particularly important to whites in the South: "Lynching allowed white southerners to perform and attach themselves to these beliefs [about white supremacy]—to literally inhabit them. The crowds of spectators at most public lynchings also literally created a community of white southerners united by a common interest and purpose" (Wood 8). The grisly photograph (reproduced but altered in *Citizen*) was a commonplace souvenir: The public spectacle of lynching was prolonged through the circulation of "displays of lynched bodies and souvenirs" and representations of violence including, "photographs and other visual imagery, ballads and songs, news accounts and lurid narratives" that were shared long after the lynching itself was over. (Wood 2)

Rankine had to obtain permission, in republishing the photograph, to alter it in this way. To study the fascination, delight, and excitement on the faces of the white spectators, who purposely went to view the lynching, can be overwhelming, even to those who have seen the photograph previously. Several of the spectators turn toward the camera and two men smile, as if posing for a family portrait. One of the men facing the camera simultaneously points toward where the Black bodies are in the original photograph, emphasizing the purpose of the gathering. The men are clean shaven; some of them wear hats and ties. Several women have also turned to face the camera. They appear to range in age from young adults to seniors. Rather than staring at the Black bodies (assuming the same role of the white spectators in the photograph) and instead looking into the faces of the assembled white crowd, readers of *Citizen* are challenged to consider the role that spectatorship plays in Black death and

Black suffering—just as the poem script about Katrina challenges us to be with the victims of the storm, rather than assuming the role of a spectator viewing/consuming their suffering on television. The distinction between being *with*, rather than looking *at*, highlights *Citizen*'s role in redefining the collective "you." Which "you" are you a part of as you view the photograph ? Who are you with in this scene?

Making the destruction of Black life uncomfortably visible, Rankine explains that Wangechi Mutu's *Sleeping Heads* (as well as Clark's *Little Girl* discussed above) "are both, in a sense, collaged pieces insisting the viewer bring together that which does not live together. They are disturbing because they are 'wrong' and yet familiar on a certain level. ... The incongruity, the dissonance, revolts and attracts" (Berlant, "Claudia Rankine by Lauren Berlant"). *Sleeping Heads* is placed in Section VII across from text which states, in part, "The worst injury is feeling you don't belong so much / to you—" (146). Like the poem script for Hurricane Katrina, Mutu's mixed media collage merges images of discarded objects (including motorcycle parts) and body parts, offering both as detritus, enacting alienation from one's body and lack of self-ownership: "you don't belong so much / to you."

Born in Kenya, Mutu discusses how people throughout Africa have been taught to "despise" their own bodies:

Being taught to despise your body is being taught to perhaps admire someone else's body more than yours—being taught that your body is good for certain things and not for others. It's good for labor, but it's not ideal if someone were to sit in a political post or something. It belongs in a certain frame and not in others and I think that was something taught to us, given to us or forced upon us.

Part of a series, all of the bodies in *Sleeping Heads* are prone (not vertical as the one reproduced in *Citizen*) and thus in this vulnerable position, described as "sleeping." In the image of the *Sleeping Head* reproduced in *Citizen*, a hand is placed across the neck so as to appear to be choking it and a small, flexed arm blocks the mouth, which appears to be biting into it (147). *Sleeping Heads* prompts viewers to consider who is eating whom in this grotesque, yet familiar, pastiche of the social body, and who benefits from current power structures and who is "eaten alive" by them. Rankine's multi-media project—across text, video, and image—asks more of its readers and viewers than it answers, pushing readers to contemplate how to disassemble and reform the individual and social body into forms that emphasize shared humanity.

Works Cited

Abrams, M. H. *A Glossary of Literary Terms*. 6th ed, Harcourt Brace Jovanovich College Publishers, 1993.

Adams, Bella. "Black Lives/White Backgrounds: Claudia Rankine's *Citizen: An American Lyric* and Critical Race Theory." *Comparative American Studies: An International Journal*, vol. 50, no. 1–2, 2017, pp. 54–71.

"Aquatint." *Tate*, https://www.tate.org.uk/art/art-terms/a/aquatint. Accessed 29 Aug. 2022.

"Attrition, n." *OED Online. Oxford English Dictionary*, Oxford UP, 2019, http://www.oed.com/view/Entry/12946. Accessed 27 June 2019.

"AWP: Values & Mission." awpwriter.org, Association of Writers and Writing Programs, 2023, https://www.awpwriter.org/about/mission. Accessed 25 Jan. 2023.

Balaev, Michelle. "Trends in Literary Trauma Theory." *Mosaic: An Interdisciplinary Critical Journal*, vol. 41, no. 2, 2008, pp. 149–66. *JSTOR*, http://www.jstor.org/stable/44029500.

Bedient, Calvin. "Review: The End of the Alphabet | Boston Review." *Boston Review*, 1 June 1999, http://bostonreview.net/poetry/calvin-bedient-review-end-alphabet. Accessed 16 Feb. 2019.

Bell, Kevin. "Unheard Writing in the Climate of Spectacular Noise: Claudia Rankine on TV." *The Global South*, vol. 3, no. 1, Spring 2009, pp. 93–107.

Bell, Susan. "Renowned Poet Claudia Rankine to Join English Department." *USC News*, 9 July 2015, https://news.usc.edu/83689/poet-claudia-rankine-to-join-english-department/. Accessed 14 April 2022.

Berlant, Lauren. "Claudia Rankine by Lauren Berlant." *BOMB Magazine*, no. 129, 1 Oct. 2014, https://bombmagazine.org/articles/claudia-rankine/.

---. *Cruel Optimism*. Duke University Press, 2011.

Blader, Bonnie. "Book Review: Plot by Claudia Rankine." *Rain Taxi*, Winter 2001/2002, http://www.raintaxi.com/plot/. Accessed 10 June 2019.

Bloch, Julia. "'Shut Your Rhetorics in a Box': Gwendolyn Brooks and Lyric Dilemma." *Tulsa Studies in Women's Literature*, vol. 35, no. 2, 2016, pp. 439–62.

Bogousslavsky, Julien, and Sebastian Dieguez. "Sigmund Freud and Hysteria: The Etiology of Psychoanalysis?" *Frontiers of Neurology and Neuroscience*, vol. 35, 2014, pp. 109–25. https://doi.org/10.1159/000360244.

Bošković, Ana, and Oliver J. Rando. "Transgenerational Epigenetic Inheritance." *Annual Review of Genetics*, vol. 52, no. 1, Nov. 2018, pp. 21–41. https://doi.org/10.1146/annurev-genet-120417-031404.

Böttiger, Helmut. "Auf der Suche nach einer graueren Sprache." *Jüdische Allgemeine*, 21 Nov. 2020, https://www.juedische-allgemeine.de/kultur/suche-nach-einer-graueren-sprache/.

Bradstreet, Anne. "The Author to Her Book by Anne Bradstreet - Poems." *poets.org,* Academy of American Poets, https://poets.org/poem/author-her-book. Accessed 12 July 2019.

Briante, Susan. "Coultas and Robertson Write the City from Surface to Detritus, from I to We." *Jacket*, vol. 36, 2008, http://jacketmagazine.com/36/briante-robertson-coultas.shtml. Accessed 8 April 2022.

Brinkley, Douglas. "The Broken Promise of the Levees That Failed New Orleans." *Smithsonian Magazine*, Sept. 2015, https://www.smithsonianmag.com/smithsonian-institution/broken-promise-levees-failed-new-orleans-180956326/. Accessed 23 Oct. 2019.

Brooks, Gwendolyn. *Blacks*. Third World Press, 1987.

---. "The Mother." *poets.org*, Academy of American Poets, https://poets.org/poem/mother. Accessed 6 Feb. 2023.

Buck, Theo. *Muttersprache, Mördersprache*. Rimbaud Verlag, 1993.

Burt, Stephen. "What Is This Thing Called Lyric?" *Modern Philology*, vol. 113, no. 3, Feb. 2016, pp. 422–40. *The University of Chicago Press Journals*, https://doi.org/10.1086/684097.

Butler, Judith. *Gender Trouble: Feminism and the Subversion of Identity*. Routledge, 1990.

Carlson, Kathryn. "An Artist's Twist on Taxidermy Blurs the Boundaries of Humanity." *National Geographic*, 24 July 2015, https://www.nationalgeographic.com/photography/article/a-twist-on-taxidermy-blurs-the-boundaries-of-humanity.

Carter, Michael T. "Reviewed Work: The End of the Alphabet by Claudia Rankine." *Ploughshares*, vol. 24, no. 1, Winter 1998/1999, pp. 222–23.

Caruth, Cathy. *Unclaimed Experience: Trauma, Narrative, and History*. Johns Hopkins University Press, 2016.

Chan, Mary-Jean. "Towards a Poetics of Racial Trauma: Lyric Hybridity in Claudia Rankine's Citizen." *Journal of American Studies*, vol. 52, no. 1, 2018, pp. 137–63.

"Charles Olson." *Poetry Foundation*, 2022, https://www.poetryfoundation.org/poets/charles-olson. Accessed 25 Feb. 2022

Childs, Peter, and Roger Fowler. *The Routledge Dictionary of Literary Terms*. Routledge, 2006. *EBSCO*, http://ezproxy.memphis.edu/login?url=https://search.ebscohost.com/login.aspx?direct=true&db=nlebk&AN=164171&site=eds-live&scope=site.

"Claudia Rankine | Academy of American Poets." *poets.org*,
    Academy of American Poets,
    https://poets.org/poet/claudia-rankine. Accessed 21 June
    2019.

"Claudia Rankine." *Poetry Foundation*,
    https://www.poetryfoundation.org/poets/claudia-rankine.
    Accessed 22 March 2019.

"Claudia Rankine on Being a Conduit for Conversation."
YouTube, uploaded by ArtsEmerson,
    27 Feb. 2018,
https://www.youtube.com/watch?v=qY97L_Kq8fk. Accessed 15
Apr.
    2022.

"Claudia Rankine on Writing *Help*." *The Shed*,
    https://theshed.org/feed_items/300?context=event&page=
    0. Accessed 19 Apr. 2022.

"Claudia Rankine Reads from Citizen at the 92nd Street Y."
YouTube, uploaded by the 92nd Street
    Y, New York, 24 Dec. 2015,
https://www.youtube.com/watch?v=8cnq71TlUvo.
    Accessed 14 August 2019.

Cocozza, Paula. "Poet Claudia Rankine: 'The Invisibility of
    Black Women Is Astounding.'"*The Guardian*, 29 June
    2015,
    https://www.theguardian.com/lifeandstyle/2015/jun/29/po
    et-claudia-rankine-invisibility-black-women-everyday-
    racism-citizen. Accessed 30 June 2018.

Cooper, Brittney. "Intersectionality." *The Oxford Handbook of
    Feminist Theory*, edited by Lisa Disch and M. E.
    Hawkesworth, Oxford UP, 2018, pp. 385–406.

Cover copy. *Nothing in Nature is Private*, by Claudia Rankine,
    Cleveland Poetry Center at Cleveland State University,
    1994.

Crater, Theresa L. "Lily Briscoe's Vision: The Articulation of Silence." *Rocky Mountain Review of Language and Literature*, vol. 50, no. 2, 1996, pp. 121–36. *JSTOR*, https://doi.org/10.2307/1348227.

Culler, Jonathan. "Extending the Theory of the Lyric." *Diacritics*, vol. 45, no. 4, 2017, pp. 6–14. *Project Muse*, https://doi.org/10.1353/dia.2017.0017.

Cvetkovich, Ann. *Depression: A Public Feeling.* Duke UP, 2012.

Delgado, Richard. "Storytelling for Oppositionists and Others: A Plea For Narrative." *Michigan Law Review*, vol. 87, Aug. 1989, pp. 2411–2441.

Dolen, Christine. "Claudia Rankine Examines Racial Privilege in GableStage's The White Card." *Miami New Times*, https://www.miaminewtimes.com/arts/interview-with-claudia-rankine-on-the-white-card-at-gablestage-13972984. Accessed 15 Apr. 2022.

Dunbar, Paul Laurence. "The Haunted Oak by Paul Laurence Dunbar." *Poetry Foundation*, https://www.poetryfoundation.org/poems/44195/the-haunted-oak. Accessed 30 Mar. 2019

---. "We Wear the Mask by Paul Laurence Dunbar." *Poetry Foundation*, https://www.poetryfoundation.org/poems/44203/we-wear-the-mask. Accessed 29 Aug. 2019.

"Efface, v." *OED Online, Oxford English Dictionary*, Oxford UP, 2019, http://www.oed.com/view/Entry/59650. Accessed 19 July 2019.

"Epigenetics & Inheritance." *Learn. Genetics*, Genetic Science Learning Center, Univ, Of Utah, 2015, https://learn.genetics.utah.edu/content/epigenetics/inheritance/. Accessed 19 Nov. 2019.

"Ersatz, n." *OED Online, Oxford English Dictionary*, Oxford UP, 2019, http://www.oed.com/view/Entry/64134. Accessed 17 June 2019.

"Exhibition Catalog: Atemwende – Making." *Edmund de Waal*, 2013, https://www.edmunddewaal.com/making/atemwende. Accessed 13 June 2022.

Exner, Richard. "Paul Celan's Atemwende: 'Death of Speech' and 'Hope of Silence.'" *Sulfur*, vol. 11, 1984, pp. 71–81.

Ferguson, Margaret W., et al., editors. *The Norton Anthology of Poetry*. Sixth edition, W. W. Norton & Company, 2018.

Foley, Abram. "Claudia Rankine, Friedrich Nietzsche, and the Untimely Present." *Symplokē*, vol. 26, no. 1–2, 2018, pp. 225–36, *JSTOR*, https://doi.org/10.5250/symploke.26.1-2.0225.

Franke, William. "Poetics of Silence in the Post-Holocaust Poetry of Paul Celan." *Journal of Literature and Trauma Studies*, vol. 2, no. 1–2, 2013, pp. 137–58.

Fraser, Alison. "Diasporic Object Lessons: Material Identity and the Korean Diaspora in the Work of Theresa Hak Kyung Cha." *WSQ: Women's Studies Quarterly*, vol. 47, no. 1–2, Spring Summer 2019, pp. 31–47.

Fraser, Kathleen. *Translating the Unspeakable: Poetry and the Innovative Necessity: Essays*. U of Alabama P, 2000.

Frost, Elisabeth A. "Claudia Rankine and the Body Politic." *The News from Poems: Essays on the 21-St Century American Poetry of Engagement*, edited by Jeffrey Gray and Ann Keniston, U of Michigan P, 2016, pp. 168–92.

Gander, Catherine. *Muriel Rukeyeser and Documentary: The Poetics of Connection*. Edinburgh UP, 2013.

Gibbens, Sarah. "Hurricane Katrina, Explained." *National Geographic*, 16 Jan. 2019, https://www.nationalgeographic.com/environment/natural-disasters/reference/hurricane-katrina/. Accessed 24 Oct. 2019.

"Glenn Ligon - Bio | The Broad."
https://www.thebroad.org/art/glenn-ligon. Accessed 30
Aug. 2022.

Goldstein, Michael. "The Other Beating." *Latimes.Com*, 19 Feb.
2006, http://www.latimes.com/la-tm-holidayfeb19-
story.html. Accessed 1 July 2018.

Gordon, Ed. "Spike Lee Produces a Vision of Katrina." *npr.org*,
18 Aug. 2006,
https://www.npr.org/templates/story/story.php?storyId=56
69697. Accessed 24 Oct. 2019.

Greene, Roland, and Stephen Cushman, editors. *The Princeton
Handbook of Poetic Terms: Third Edition*. Princeton UP,
2016. *JSTOR*, https://doi.org/10.2307/j.ctvcszz59.

Hahamy, Madison, and Emily Tian. "Claudia Rankine to Depart
Yale for NYU next Year." *Yale Daily News*, 22 Oct. 2020,
https://yaledailynews.com/blog/2020/10/22/claudia-
rankine-to-depart-yale-for-nyu-next-year/. Accessed 21
Aug. 2022.

Hanisch, Carol. "The Personal Is Political: The Women's
Liberation Movement Classic with a New Explanatory
Introduction." *Carolhanisch.Org*, Feb. 1969. Accessed 9
Oct. 2019.

Hartman, Saidiya V. *Lose Your Mother: A Journey along the
Atlantic Slave Route*. Farrar, Straus & Giroux, 2008.

"Help: A New Play by Claudia Rankine." *The Shed*,
https://theshed.org/program/225-help-a-new-play-by-
claudia-rankine. Accessed 11 Apr. 2022.

History.com Editors. "Million Man March." *HISTORY*, 21 Sept.
2021, https://www.history.com/this-day-in-
history/million-man-march-1995. Accessed 19 Aug. 2022.

Horne, Jed. "Five Myths about Hurricane Katrina." *Washington
Post*, 31 Aug. 2012. *www.washingtonpost.com*,
https://www.washingtonpost.com/opinions/five-myths-

about-hurricane-katrina/2012/08/31/003f4064-f147-11e1-a612-3cfc842a6d89_story.html. Accessed 23 Oct. 2019.

Houen, Alex. "Reckoning Sacrifice in 'War on Terror' Literature." *Sacrifice and Modern War Literature: The Battle of Waterloo to the War on Terror*, edited by Alex Houen and Jan-Melissa Schramm, Oxford UP, 2018, pp. 237–54.

Hume, Angela. "Toward an Antiracist Ecopoetics: Waste and Wasting in the Poetry of Claudia Rankine." *Contemporary Literature*, vol. 57, no. 1, Spring 2016, pp. 79–110.

Hunt, Erica. "All About You." *Los Angeles Review of Books*, 8 Dec. 2014, https://lareviewofbooks.org/article/all-about-you/. Accessed 13 Nov. 2019.

Hunt, Erica, and Dawn Lundy Martin, editors. *Letters to the Future: Black Women: Radical Writing*. Kore Press, 2018.

"Inverse, Adj. and n." *OED Online, Oxford English Dictionary*, Oxford UP, 2019, http://www.oed.com/view/Entry/99001. Accessed 18 June 2019.

Isherwood, Charles. "Have You Ever Visited the Broncks?" *New York Times*, New York, 17 Sept. 2009, p. C3.

Jack, Peter Monro. "'Land of the Free' Is a Grim and Beautiful Masterpiece of Collaboration." *New York Times*, 8 May 1939, p. 94.

Jackson, Virginia. *Dickinson's Misery: A Theory of Lyric Reading*. Princeton UP, 2005.

Jenckes, Kate. "Generation." *Diacritics*, vol. 49, no. 2, 2021, pp. 93–99. *Project Muse*, https://doi.org/10.1353/dia.2021.0017.

Jenkins, Amber. "Drafting Mrs. Ramsay and Lily Briscoe: Visual Aesthetics and the Manuscript of Virginia Woolf's To the Lighthouse." *Woolf Studies Annual*, vol. 27, 2021, p. 5+. *Gale Academic OneFile*,

https://link.gale.com/apps/doc/A707651789/AONE?u=tel
_s_tsla&sid=bookmark-AONE&xid=b3b41063.

Johnson, Barbara. *A World of Difference*. John Hopkins
University Press, 1989.

Joris, Pierre. "Introduction." *Paul Celan: Selections*, U of
California P, 2005, pp. 3–36.

Keller, Lynn. *Forms of Expansion: Recent Long Poems by
Women*. U of Chicago P, 1997.

Kimberley, Emma. "Politics and Poetics of Fear after 9/11:
Claudia Rankine's Don't Let Me Be Lonely." *Journal of
American Studies*, vol. 45, no. 4, Nov. 2011, pp. 777–791.

King, Helen. "Once Upon a Text: Hysteria from Hippocrates."
Hysteria Beyond Freud, by Sander L.Gilman, Helen King,
Roy Porter, G. S. Rousseau, and Elaine Showalter, U of
California P, 1993, pp. 3–90.

Koestenbaum, Wayne. "Strange and Admirable." *Parnassus:
Poetry in Review*, vol. 24, no. 2, 2000, pp. 297–311.

Krasny, Elke. "Hysteria Activism: Feminist Collectives for the
Twenty-First Century." *Performing Hysteria*, edited by
Johanna Braun, Leuven University Press, 2020, pp. 125–
46, *JSTOR*, https://doi.org/10.2307/j.ctv18dvt2d.10.

Lange, Dorothea, and Paul Taylor. *An American Exodus: A
Record of Human Erosion*. Reynal & Hitchcock, 1939.

Lee, Felicia R. "A Poetry Personal and Political." *The New York
Times*, 28 Nov. 2014. *NYTimes.com*,
https://www.nytimes.com/2014/11/29/books/claudia-
rankine-on-citizen-and-racial-politics.html. Accessed 24
June 2019.

Lewis, Cara. "Still Life in Motion: Mortal Form in Woolf's *To
the Lighthouse*." *Twentieth-Century Literature*, vol. 60,
no. 4, Dec. 2014, pp. 423–54. *JSTOR*,
https://doi.org/10.1215/0041462X-2014-1001.

Ligon, Glenn. *Untitled (Four Etchings)*. 1992, *Cleveland Museum of Art*, https://www.clevelandart.org/art/1994.159.

Ligon, Glenn. *Untitled: Four Etchings*. 1992, *The Metropolitan Museum of Art*, https://www.metmuseum.org/art/collection/search/490241. Accessed 29 Aug. 2022.

Ligon, Glenn. *Untitled (Speech/Crowd) #3*. 2000, *The Studio Museum in Harlem*, https://studiomuseum.org/collection-item/untitled-speechcrowd-3.

Lorde, Audre. "The Master's Tools Will Never Dismantle the Master's House." *Sister Outsider: Essays and Speeches*. Crossing Press, 1984. pp. 110-113.

---. "Poetry Is Not a Luxury." *Sister Outsider: Essays and Speeches*, Crossing Press, 1984, pp. 36–39.

Louth, Charlie. "Snow Part/Schneepart. By Paul Celan. Translated by Ian Fairley. Pp xxvi+195. Manchester." *Translation and Literature*, vol. 17, no. 2, Sept. 2008, pp. 261–67. *Edinburgh University Press Journals*, https://doi.org/10.3366/E0968136108000320.

Lucas, John, director. "August 29, 2005/Hurricane Katrina." *Vimeo*, 8 Oct. 2015, https://vimeo.com/141818727. Accessed 30 Dec. 2019.

---. "Claudia Rankine's Poem 'Stop and Frisk.'" *YouTube*, 4 Dec. 2014, https://www.youtube.com/watch?v=kN5aYIrc2J8. Accessed 18 Aug. 2022.

MacLeish, Archibald. *A Time to Speak: The Selected Prose of Archibald MacLeish*. Houghton Mifflin, 1940.

Macmillan, Rebecca. "The Archival Poetics of Claudia Rankine's Don't Let Me Be Lonely: An American Lyric." *Contemporary Literature*, vol. 58, no. 2, Summer 2017, pp. 173–203.

Melhem, D. H. *Gwendolyn Brooks: Poetry & the Heroic Voice*. UP of Kentucky, 1987.

Meyerhofer, Nicholas J. "Ambiguities of Interpretation: Translating the Late Celan." *Studies in 20th & 21st Century Literature*, vol. 8, no. 1, Sept. 1983, pp. 9–22. https://doi.org/10.4148/2334-4415.1129.

Mikics, David. *A New Handbook of Literary Terms*. Yale UP, 2007.

"The Million Man March." *Amistad Digital Resource*, 2009, https://www.amistadresource.org/the_future_in_the_present/the_million_man_march.html. Acessed 19 August 2022.

Mitchell, Koritha. *Living with Lynching: African American Lynching Plays, Performance, and Citizenship, 1890-1930*. U of Illinois P, 2012.

Morrison, Derrilyn E. "GPA Annual Meeting Keynote Address: Crossing the Line: Caribbean Poets in America." *Journal of the Georgia Philological Association*, vol. 6, 2017 2016, pp. 5–9.

Moya, Paula M. L. *Learning From Experience: Minority Identities, Multicultural Struggles*. U of California P, 2002.

Mutu, Wangechi. "Artist Wangechi Mutu: 'My Lab Is the Female Body.'" Interview by Isha Sesay. *CNN: African Voices*, 19 July 2011, http://www.cnn.com/2011/WORLD/africa/07/19/wangechi.mutu.artist/index.html. Accessed 30 Dec. 2019.

Newcomer, Caitlin E. "Casting a Shadow from Flesh to Canvas: Claudia Rankine's Plot and the Gendered Textual Body." *GENRE*, vol. 47, no. 3, 2014, pp. 357–77.

Nielsen, Aldon Lynn, and Lauri Scheyer, editors. *Every Goodbye Ain't Gone: An Anthology of Innovative Poetry by African Americans*. U of Alabama P, 2006.

---. *What I Say: Innovative Poetry by Black Writers in America*. U of Alabama P, 2015.

Nietzsche, Friedrich Wilhelm. *Untimely Meditations*. Translated by R. J. Hollingdale, Cambridge UP, 1997.

Nieuwenhuis, Marijn. "Celan, Paul." *Global Social Theory*, https://globalsocialtheory.org/thinkers/celan-paul/. Accessed 25 Jan. 2023.

Oakley, Seanna Sumalee. *Common Places: The Poetics of African Atlantic Postromantics*. Rodopi, 2011.

Olson, Charles. "Projective Verse by Charles Olson." *Poetry Foundation*, https://www.poetryfoundation.org/articles/69406/projective-verse. Accessed 25 Feb. 2022.

Ortiz, Erik. "George Holliday, Who Taped Rodney King Beating, Urges Others to Share Videos." *NBC News*, 9 June 2015, https://www.nbcnews.com/nightly-news/george-holliday-who-taped-rodney-king-beating-urges-others-share-n372551. Accessed 1 July 2018.

"Our History – Timeline." *Treatment Action Campaign*, https://www.tac.org.za/our-history/. Accessed 14 July 2020.

Perelman, Bob. "Parataxis and Narrative: The New Sentence in Theory and Practice." *American Literature*, vol. 65, no. 2, June 1993, pp. 313–24. *JSTOR*, https://doi.org/10.2307/2927344.

"Poetry Book Review: *PLOT* by Claudia Rankine." *PublishersWeekly.Com*, 19 Feb. 2001, https://www.publishersweekly.com/9780802137920. 14 June 2019.

Proudfit, Sharon Wood. "Lily Briscoe's Painting: A Key to Personal Relationships in 'To the Lighthouse.'" *Criticism*, vol. 13, no. 1, 1971, pp. 26–38. *JSTOR*, http://www.jstor.org/stable/23098980.

Rankine, Claudia. "Adrienne Rich's Poetic Transformations." *The New Yorker*, 12 May 2016. *www.newyorker.com*, https://www.newyorker.com/books/page-turner/adrienne-richs-poetic-transformations. Accessed 20 Aug. 2022.

---. *Citizen: An American Lyric*. Graywolf Press, 2014.

---. "Claudia Rankine." Interview by Katie Lederer. *The Verse Book of Interviews: 27 Poets on Language, Craft & Culture*, edited by Brian Henry and Andrew Zawacki, Verse Press, 2005, pp. 147–51.

---. *Don't Let Me Be Lonely: An American Lyric*. Graywolf Press, 2004.

---. *Nothing in Nature Is Private*. Cleveland Poetry Center at Cleveland State University, 1994.

---."On Being Seen: An Interview with Claudia Rankine from Ferguson." Interview by
Alexandra Schwartz. *www.newyorker.com*, 22 Aug. 2014, https://www.newyorker.com/books/page-turner/seen-interview-claudia-rankine-ferguson.
Accessed 19 Dec. 2019.

---. *Plot*. Grove Press, 2001.

---. "Poetry Daily Prose Feature: Interview by Claudia Rankine by Jennifer Flescher and Robert N. Caspar." *Poetry Daily*. http://poems.com/special_features/prose/essay_rankine.php. Accessed 12 June 2018.

---. *The End of the Alphabet*. Grove Press, 1998.

---. "The History Behind the Feeling: A Conversation with Claudia Rankine by Aaron Coleman." *The Spectacle*, 23 Sept. 2015, https://thespectacle.wustl.edu/?p=105. Accessed 29 March 2020.

---. Rankine, Claudia, Beth Loffreda, and Cap Max King. *The Racial Imaginary: Writers on Race in the Life of the Mind*. Fence Books, 2015.

Rankine, Claudia, and John Lucas. "Situation 5, by Claudia Rankine and John Lucas." *YouTube*, 26 July 2011, https://www.youtube.com/watch?v=0xx1dwFxAv0. Accessed 24 July 2019.

---. "Whiteness, Inc." *Artforum International*, vol. 54, no. 10, 2016, pp. 368–69.

Robbins, Amy Moorman. *American Hybrid Poetics: Gender, Mass Culture, and Form*. Rutgers UP, 2014.

Roeder, Amy. "The Cost of South Africa's Misguided AIDS Policies." *Harvard T. H. Chan School of Public Health News Magazine*, 15 May 2009. https://www.hsph.harvard.edu/news/magazine/spr09aids/. Accessed 14 July 2020.

Rukeyser, Muriel. *The Life of Poetry*. 1st ed, Paris Press, 1996.

---. "'We Aren't Sure...We're Wondering.' Review of Land of the Free by Archibald MacLeish." *New Masses*, vol. XXVII, no. 5, Apr. 1938, pp. 26–28.

Sastry, Anjul, and Karen Grigsby Bates. "When LA Erupted In Anger: A Look Back At The Rodney King Riots." *npr.org*, 26 Apr. 2017, https://www.npr.org/2017/04/26/524744989/when-la-erupted-in-anger-a-look-back-at-the-rodney-king-riots. Accessed 30 June 2018.

Scheck, Frank. "Bronx Bus-Ride 'Beauty' Is Just the Ticket." *New York Post*, 18 Sept. 2009, https://nypost.com/2009/09/18/bronx-bus-ride-beauty-is-just-the-ticket/. Accessed 10 Oct. 2019.

Schwendener, Martha, et al. "What to See in New York Art Galleries This Week." *The New York Times*, 8 Aug. 2018, https://www.nytimes.com/2018/08/08/arts/design/what-to-see-in-new-york-art-galleries-this-week.html. Accessed 28 June 2019.

Serafin, Steven R. "Claudia Rankine | Jamaican-Born Poet, Playwright, Educator, and Multimedia Artist." *Encyclopedia Britannica*, https://www.britannica.com/biography/Claudia-Rankine. Accessed 20 June 2019.

Shockley, Evie. *Renegade Poetics: Black Aesthetics and Formal Innovation in African American Poetry*. U of Iowa P, 2011.

Skillman, Nikki. "Lyric Reading Revisited: Passion, Address, and Form in Citizen." *American Literary History*, vol. 31, no. 3, 2019, pp. 419–57.

Smethurst, James. "Paul Laurence Dunbar and Turn-into-the-20th-Century African American Dualism." *African American Review*, vol. 41, no. 2, 2007, pp. 377–86.

Sontag, Susan. *On Photography*. Farrar, Straus and Giroux, 1977.

Spears, Brian. "An Open Letter from Claudia Rankine." *The Rumpus.Net*, 12 Feb. 2011, https://therumpus.net/2011/02/12/an-open-letter-from-claudia-rankine/. Accessed 21 Aug. 2022.

Steiner, George. *After Babel: Aspects of Language and Translation*. Oxford UP, 1975.

"Stop and Frisk." *LII / Legal Information Institute*, https://www.law.cornell.edu/wex/stop_and_frisk. Accessed 18 Aug. 2022.

Stott, William. *Documentary Expression and Thirties America*. U of Chicago P, 1986.

"Sugar Lift Etching." Leichester Print Workshop, http://www.leicesterprintworkshop.com/files/uploads/sugar_lift_etching.pdf. Accessed 29 Aug. 2022.

The Ingmar Bergman Foundation. "Scenes from a Marriage." *Ingmar Bergman*, https://www.ingmarbergman.se/en/production/scenes-marriage. Accessed 12 June 2019.

---. "Wild Strawberries." *Ingmar Bergman*, https://www.ingmarbergman.se/en/production/wild-strawberries. Accessed 12 June 2019.

"The L.A. Riots: 15 Years After Rodney King - TIME." *Time*, 27 Apr. 2007. *content.time.com*, http://content.time.com/time/specials/2007/la_riot/article/

0,28804,1614117_1614084_1614511,00.html. 3 July 2018.

Thompson, Taahira. "NYPD's Infamous Stop-and-Frisk Policy Found Unconstitutional." *The Leadership Conference Education Fund*, 21 Aug. 2013, https://civilrights.org/edfund/resource/nypds-infamous-stop-and-frisk-policy-found-unconstitutional/. Accessed 18 August 2022.

Tiffany, Daniel. "Lyric Poetry and Poetics." *Oxford Research Encyclopedia of Literature*, Oxford UP, 2020. *Oxford Research Encyclopedias*, https://doi.org/10.1093/acrefore/9780190201098.013.111 1.

---. "Speaking in Tongues: Poetry and the Residues of Shared Language." *Tupelo Quarterly*, 14 Mar. 2020, https://www.tupeloquarterly.com/prose/speaking-in-tongues-poetry-and-the-residues-of-shared-language/. Accessed 24 Jan. 2023.

"Today in History - August 29-Hurricane Katrina." *Library of Congress, Washington, D.C. 20540 USA*, https://www.loc.gov/item/today-in-history/august-29/. Accessed 30 Dec. 2019.

van der Kolk, Bessel. "The Body Keeps The Score." *Bessel van Der Kolk, MD.*, https://www.besselvanderkolk.com/resources/the-body-keeps-the-score. Accessed 3 Feb. 2023.

Welch, Tana Jean. "Don't Let Me Be Lonely : The Trans-Corporeal Ethics of Claudia Rankine's Investigative Poetics." *MELUS: Multi-Ethnic Literature of the United States*, vol. 40, no. 1, 2015, pp. 124–48. *Project Muse*. http://ezproxy.memphis.edu/login?url=http://search.ebsco host.com/login.aspx?direct=true&db=edspmu&AN=edsp mu.S194631701510009X&site=eds-live&scope=site

Westervelt, Eric. "In 'Citizen,' Poet Strips Bare The Realities Of Everyday Racism." *npr.org*, 3 Jan. 2015, https://www.npr.org/2015/01/03/374574142/in-citizen-poet-strips-bare-the-realities-of-everyday-racism.

What Is Epigenetics? Center on the Developing Child, Harvard University, https://harvardcenter.wpenginepowered.com/wp-content/uploads/2019/02/EpigeneticsInfographic_FINAL.pdf. Accessed 1 Feb. 2023.

"What Is Narrative Theory? | Project Narrative." *Project Narrative*, https://projectnarrative.osu.edu/about/what-is-narrative-theory. Accessed 3 Feb. 2023.

The White Card | Graywolf Press. https://www.graywolfpress.org/books/white-card. Accessed 19 Apr. 2022.

"The Whiteness Issue." *The Racial Imaginary Institute*, Sept. 2017, https://theracialimaginary.org/about/. Accessed 26 April 2019.

Williams, Patricia J. "On Being the Object of Property." *Signs*, vol. 14, no. 1, 1988, pp. 5–24.

Wood, Amy Louise. *Lynching and Spectacle: Witnessing Racial Violence in America, 1890-1940*. University of North Carolina Press, 2009, *EBSCO*, search.ebscohost.com.ezproxy.memphis.edu/login.aspx?direct=true&db=nlebk&AN=354831&site=eds-live&scope=site.

Woolf, Virginia. *To the Lighthouse*. Macmillan Collector's Library, 1927.